Baking for Beg

Quick and Easy, Proven Recipes

**FLAME TREE
PUBLISHING**

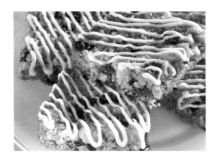 

Contents

Essential Ingredients..12

Equipment 17

Basic Techniques 22

Basic Recipes: Pastry...27

Basic Recipes: Batters..30

Basic Recipes: Meringues 31

Basic Recipes: Icings..32

Culinary Terms Explained...36

Useful Conversions..40

Classic Cakes & Bakes 42

Anyone who wants to bake cakes inevitably needs to know how to make a basic sponge – so many cakes take their cues from this. However, believe it or not, it can be tricky to create a perfectly cooked, light Victoria sponge. This section provides an easy recipe for this classic cake along with a whole range of essential standards and simple recipes, such as Carrot Cake, Fruit Cake, Coffee & Pecan Cake and even every child's favourite – Crispy Rice Cakes.

Easy Victoria Sponge 44
Fat-free Sponge 46
Carrot Cake 48
Banana Cake 50
Fruit Cake..52

*⁀ **Chocolate alternative: Fruit & Spice
Chocolate Slice, page 100***

Dundee Cake 54
Christmas Cake..56
Lemon Drizzle Cake 58
Orange Fruit Cake 60
Toffee Apple Cake 62
Honey Cake 64
Almond Cake...66
Gingerbread 68
Drop Scones 70
Easy Danish Pastries 72
Jammy Buns 74
Chestnut Cake 76
Crispy Rice Cakes 78
Easy Chocolate Cake 80
Marble Cake 82
Coffee & Pecan Cake 84

*⁀ **Coconut alternative: Moist Mocha & Coconut Cake,
page 88***

Chocolate Pecan Traybake 86
Moist Mocha & Coconut Cake 88
All-in-one Chocolate Fudge Cakes 90
Chocolate Nut Brownies..92
Chocolate & Orange Rock Buns.......................................94
Butterscotch Loaf 96
Marmalade Loaf Cake 98
Fruit & Spice Chocolate Slice 100

Cupcakes & Muffins 102

The fun alternative to classic cakes are beautiful and enticing individual cupcakes, or chunky, moreish muffins. Here, learn how to create delicate sponge Raspberry Butterfly Cupcakes or decadent Chocolate Fudge Flake Cupcakes; or have some fun with colours and shapes by making Fondant Fancies or Polka Dot Cupcakes. For a classic muffin that you just want to get your teeth into, try Chocolate Chip Cherry Muffins.

Madeleine Cupcakes 104
Double Cherry Cupcakes 106

Muffin alternative: Chocolate Chip Cherry Muffins, page 142

Raspberry Butterfly Cupcakes 108
Fondant Fancies...110
Almond & Cherry Cupcakes 112
Shaggy Coconut Cupcakes 114
Coffee & Walnut Fudge Cupcakes..................................116
Chocolate Mud Cupcakes 118
Chocolate Fudge Flake Cupcakes 120
Chocolate & Cranberry Cupcakes 122
Chocolate & Toffee Cupcakes 124

Cappuccino Muffins 126
Triple Chocolate Muffins 128
Orange Drizzle Cupcakes 130

Lemon alternative: Lemon Drizzle Cake, page 58

Colourful Letters Cupcakes...132
Boys' & Girls' Names 134
Jellybean Cupcakes 136
Polka Dot Cupcakes 138
Pistachio Muffins...140
Chocolate Chip Cherry Muffins 142

Biscuits & Cookies...144

Why not make your own biscuits to have with your tea? Here, you have got a raft of essential recipes that every baker should know, from cookies, such as Oatmeal Raisin Cookies and Chocolate Chip Cookies, to classic melt-in-the-mouth shortbread-type biscuits such as Viennese Fingers; from fun jammy Traffic Lights and three kinds of macaroon, to flapjacks and gingerbread – which will you choose first?

Traffic Lights 146

Cherry Garlands 148

Lemon Butter Biscuits 150

Oatmeal Raisin Cookies.................................152

❧ Plainer alternative: Melting Moments, page 156

Oatmeal Coconut Cookies...............................154

Melting Moments 156

Chocolate Chip Cookies..................................158

White Chocolate Cookies 160

Chocolate & Vanilla Rings 162

Peanut Butter Truffle Cookies.........................164

Chewy Choc & Nut Cookies............................166

Fudgy Chocolate Tiffin Bars 168

Miracle Bars 170

Golden Honey Fork Biscuits 172

Honey & Chocolate Hearts.............................174

Almond Macaroons.......................................176

Coconut Macaroons......................................178

Whipped Shortbread......................................180

❧ Decadent alternative: Pecan Caramel Millionaire's
   Shortbread, page 186

Viennese Fingers..182

Shortbread Thumbs.......................................184

Pecan Caramel Millionaire's Shortbread 186

Gingerbread Biscuits 188

Ginger Snaps 190

Chocolate & Ginger Florentines 192

Classic Flapjacks..194

Fruit & Nut Flapjacks 196

Chocolate Orange Biscuits 198

Chocolate Macaroons....................................200

Sweet Pies & Puddings................................202

No meal is complete without a dessert and, here, we have a tempting selection of baked puddings and delicious pastry desserts. Again, every baking beginner should know the classics, such as Apple Pie, crumble (rhubarb in this case), Lemon Meringue Pie and cheesecake, but then there are so many other delights to try, such as the fun 'Mars' Bar Mousse in Filo Cups or chocolate versions of classics, such as Chocolate Brioche Bake (but you may want to make the Bread & Butter Pudding first!).

Apple Pie 204

Crunchy Rhubarb Crumble.............................206

Rhubarb & Raspberry Cobbler 208

Freeform Fruit Pie..210

Classic Apple Strudel 212

❧ Pudding alternative: Baked Apple Dumplings, page 262

Mini Pistachio & Chocolate Strudels 214

'Mars' Bar Mousse in Filo Cups 216

Lemon Meringue Pie...218

Banoffee Pie...220

Ricotta Cheesecake with Strawberry Coulis..................222

Baked Lemon & Sultana Cheesecake 224

Triple Chocolate Cheesecake 226

Fudgy Mocha Pie with Espresso Custard Sauce.............228

Mini Strawberry Tartlets...230

Goats' Cheese & Lemon Tart 232

**﮳ Savoury alternative: Potato & Goats' Cheese Tart,
page 318**

Autumn Tart...234

Almond & Pine Nut Tart 236

Lattice Treacle Tart..238

Iced Bakewell Tart...240

Chocolate Pecan Pie..242

Chocolate Apricot Linzer Torte 244

Caramelised Chocolate Tartlets....................................246

Chocolate Fruit Pizza 248

Chocolate Lemon Tartlets 250

Chocolate Pecan Angel Pie...252

Bread & Butter Pudding 254

Chocolate Brioche Bake..256

Peach & Chocolate Bake 258

Luxury Mince Pies 260

Puff Pastry Jalousie...262

Baked Apple Dumplings 264

Eve's Pudding 266

Golden Castle Pudding...268

College Pudding 270

Basic Breads & Scones 272

There is nothing quite like the aroma of freshly made bread filling your kitchen, and nothing beats the satisfaction of tucking into your home-baked loaf. Start with a Quick Brown Bread or Classic White Loaf, then mix things up with Wholemeal Walnut Bread, or make some Tomato & Basil Rolls to have with dinner. Do not forget breads such as focaccia, chapatti and naan, to go with a world of dishes; and then there are the homely Hot Cross Buns and Traditional Oven Scones, or try our tea breads – perfect for that afternoon nibble with a cuppa!

Quick Brown Bread...274

Classic White Loaf..276

Multigrain Bread..278

Wholemeal Walnut Bread 280

❧ **Sweet alternative: Coffee & Walnut Fudge Cupcakes, page 116**

Irish Soda Bread 282

Soft Dinner Rolls 284

Tomato & Basil Rolls 286

Sweet Potato Baps 288

Poppy Seed Plait 290

Rosemary & Olive Focaccia......................292

❧ **Pastry alternative: Olive & Feta Parcels, page 324**

Chapattis..294

Spicy Filled Naan Bread 296

Hot Cross Buns......................................298

Traditional Oven Scones 300

Cheese-crusted Potato Scones..................302

Banana & Honey Tea Bread 304

Fruity Apple Tea Bread 306

Savoury Baking 308

Last but not least, we have got some savoury recipes for you to try your hand at – 'baking' does not just mean cakes! All ages will adore the essential Sausage Rolls and no baking book is complete without a Classic Quiche Lorraine. Have a go at making your own pizza – we've got three to choose from – so satisfying! Or if you need something a bit meatier, there are the classic Cornish Pasties and Beef & Red Wine Pie.

Sausage Rolls..310

Bacon, Mushroom & Cheese Puffs..............312

Classic Quiche Lorraine 314

❧ **Fish alternative: Smoked Salmon Quiche, page 336**

Tomato & Courgette Herb Tart......................316

Potato & Goats' Cheese Tart 318

Garlic Wild Mushroom Galettes 320

Mediteranean Tartlets...............................322

Olive & Feta Parcels 324

Three-Tomato Pizzas 326

Spinach, Pine Nut & Mascarpone Pizza.........328

Roquefort, Parma & Rocket Pizza 330

Spicy Vegetable Slice...............................332

Smoked Haddock Tart 334

Smoked Salmon Quiche............................336

Smoked Mackerel Vol-au-Vents 338

Sauvignon Chicken & Mushroom Filo Pie 340

❧ **Beef alternative: Beef & Red Wine Pie, page 348**

Moroccan Lamb with Apricots......................342

Cornish Pasties......................................344

Caribbean Empanadas.............................346

Beef & Red Wine Pie 348

Index···350

Essential Ingredients

The quantities may differ, but basic baking ingredients do not vary greatly. Let us take a look at the baking ingredients which are essential.

Fat

Butter and firm block margarine are the fats most commonly used in baking. Others can also be used such as white vegetable fat, lard and oil. Low-fat spreads are not

recommended as they break down when cooked at a high temperature. Often, it is a matter of personal preference which fat you choose when baking, but there are a few guidelines that are important to remember.

Butter and Margarine

Butter is the fat most commonly used in cake-making, especially in rich fruit cakes and the heavier sponge cakes such as Madeira or chocolate torte; it gives a distinctive flavour to the cake. You can use unsalted butter in delicate cakes and icings, but ordinary salted butter or slightly salted is better for general baking. Some people favour margarine which imparts little or no flavour to the cake. As a rule, firm margarine and butter should not be used straight from the refrigerator but allowed to come to room temperature before using (known as 'softened'). Also, it should be beaten by itself first before creaming or rubbing in. Soft margarine, sold in tubs, is a quick and easy fat that can be used straight from the refrigerator and is ideal for one-stage recipes.

Oil

Light oils, such as vegetable or sunflower, are sometimes used instead of solid fats. However, if oil is used, care should be taken – it is vital to follow a specific recipe as the proportions of oil to flour and eggs are different and these recipes will need extra raising agents.

Fat in Pastry-making

Fat is an integral ingredient when making pastry; again, there are a few specific guidelines to bear in mind. For shortcrust pastry, the best results are achieved by using equal amounts of lard or white vegetable fat with butter or block margarine. The amount of fat used is always half the amount of flour. Other pastries use differing amounts of ingredients. Pâte sucrée (a sweet flan pastry) uses all butter with eggs and a little sugar, while flaky or puff pastry uses a larger proportion of fat to flour and relies on the folding and rolling during making to ensure that the pastry rises and flakes well. When using a recipe, refer to the instructions to obtain the best result.

Flour

Flour Types

We can buy a wide range of flour, all designed for specific jobs. Strong ('bread') flour, which is rich in gluten, whether it is white (shown top left of the picture here) or brown (this includes wholemeal – shown top right – granary and stoneground) is best kept for bread.

00 flour is designed for pasta-making and there is no substitute for this flour.

Ordinary plain flour is best for cakes, biscuits and sauces as it absorbs the fat easily and gives a soft light texture. This flour comes in plain white, self-raising (which has the raising agent already incorporated, shown bottom left of the picture here) and wholemeal varieties (wholemeal self-raising, shown bottom right). Plain flour can be used for all types of baking and sauces.

Flour and Raising Agents

If using plain flour for scones or cakes and puddings, unless otherwise stated in the recipe, use 1 teaspoon baking powder to 225 g/8 oz plain flour. With sponge cakes and light fruit cakes, where it is important that an even rise is achieved, it is best to use self-raising flour because, since the raising agent has already been added, there is no danger of using too much – which can result in a sunken cake with a sour taste. There are other raising agents that are also used. Some cakes use bicarbonate of soda with or without cream of tartar (both these compounds are typical ingredients in baking powder), blended with warm or sour milk. Whisked eggs also act as a raising agent as the air trapped in the egg ensures that the mixture rises. Generally, no other raising agent is required.

Other Flours

There is even a special light sponge flour designed especially for whisked sponges. Also, it is possible to buy flours that contain no gluten and so cater for coeliacs. Buckwheat, soya, rice and chick pea flours are also available.

Eggs

When a recipe states 1 egg, it is generally accepted this refers to a medium egg. Over the past few years, the grading of eggs has changed. For years, in the UK, eggs were sold as small, standard and large, then this method changed and they were graded in numbers with 1 being the largest. The general feeling by the public was that this system was misleading, so now we buy our eggs as small, medium and large. Due to the slight risk of salmonella, all eggs are now sold date-stamped to ensure

that the eggs are used in their prime. This applies even to farm eggs which are no longer allowed to be sold straight from the farm. Look for the lion quality stamp (on 75 per cent of all eggs sold) which guarantees that the eggs come from hens vaccinated against salmonella, have been laid in the

UK and are produced to the highest food safety and standards. All of these eggs carry a best before date.

Sizes

Do remember that 'value' or 'economy' eggs may be ungraded and of different sizes, so, for best results, buy eggs marked as 'medium' and 'large'. If you do use economy eggs, make sure to note the sizes you are using and try to even out the quantity by, say, using 1 large and 2 small eggs instead of 3 medium-sized ones.

Types

There are many types of eggs sold and it really is a question of personal preference which ones are chosen. All offer the same nutritional benefits. More than half of the eggs sold in the UK are from caged hens. These are the cheapest eggs, from hens who have been fed on a manufactured mixed diet. Barn eggs are from hens kept in barns who are free to roam within the barn. However, their diet is similar to caged hens and the barns may be overcrowded.

Free-range

It is commonly thought that free-range eggs are from hens that lead a much more natural life and are fed natural foods. This, however, is not always the case and in some instances they may still live in a crowded environment and fed the same foods as caged and barn hens. However, it is good that the production of eggs from caged hens is steadily decreasing in favour of free-range eggs – with more and more shops selling only free-range.

Four-grain and Organic

Four-grain eggs are from hens that have been fed on grain and no preventative medicines have been included in their diet. Organic eggs are from hens that live in a flock, whose beaks are not clipped and who are completely free to roam. Obviously, these eggs are much more expensive than the others.

Storage

Store eggs in the refrigerator with the round end uppermost (as packed in the egg boxes). Allow to come to room temperature before using. Do remember, raw or semi-cooked eggs should not be given to babies, toddlers, pregnant women, the elderly and those suffering from a recurring illness.

Separating Eggs

When separating eggs (that is, separating the white from the yolk), crack an egg in half lightly and cleanly over a bowl, being careful not to break the yolk and keeping the yolk in the shell. Then tip the yolk backwards

and forwards between the two shell halves, allowing as much of the white as possible to spill out into the bowl. Keep or discard the yolk and/or the white as needed. Make sure that you do not get any yolk in your whites as this will prevent successful whisking of the whites. It takes practice!

Sugar

Sugar not only offers taste to baking but also adds texture and volume to the mixture. It is generally accepted that caster sugar is best for sponge cakes, puddings and meringues. Its fine granules disperse evenly when creaming or whisking. Granulated sugar is used for more general cooking, such as stewing fruit, whereas demerara sugar, with its toffee taste and crunchy texture, is good for sticky puddings and cakes such as flapjacks. For rich fruit cakes, Christmas puddings and cakes, use the muscovado sugars (soft dark brown or golden brown), which give a rich intense molasses or treacle flavour.

Icing sugar is used primarily for icings and can be used in meringues and in fruit sauces when the sugar needs to dissolve quickly.

For a different flavour, try flavouring your own sugar, for example with vanilla. Place a vanilla pod in a screw-top jar, fill with caster sugar, screw down the lid and leave for 2–3 weeks before using. Top up with more sugar after use. You can also use thinly pared lemon or orange zest in the same manner.

Reducing Sugar Intake

If trying to reduce sugar intake, then use the unrefined varieties, such as golden granulated, golden caster, unrefined demerara and the muscovado sugars. All of these are a little sweeter than their refined counterparts, so less is required. Alternatively, clear honey or fructose (fruit sugar) can reduce sugar intake as they have similar calories to sugar, but are twice as sweet. Also, they have a slow release, so their effect lasts longer. Dried fruits can also be included in the diet to top up sugar intake.

Yeast

There is something very comforting about the aroma of freshly baked bread and the taste is far different and

superior to commercially made bread. Bread-making is regarded by some as being a time-consuming process but, with the advent of fast-acting yeast, this no longer applies. There are three types of yeast available: fresh yeast, granular dried yeast (which is available in tins) and fast-action yeast powder, which comes in separate sachets in packets.

Fresh

Fresh yeast is rarely sold as a block any more. Commercial baker's yeast is now sold in a liquid form and is not easily available for the general public to buy. If you do manage to find firm fresh yeast, it should be bought in small quantities (although it freezes well); it has a putty-like colour and texture with a slight wine smell. It should be creamed with a little sugar and some warm liquid before being added to the flour. If you have liquid yeast, just sprinkle on sugar and stir. However, dried yeast is much easier to find and use.

Dried

Dried yeast can be stored for up to six months and comes in small hard granules. It should be sprinkled onto lukewarm liquid with a little sugar, then left to stand, normally between 15–20 minutes, until the mixture froths. When replacing fresh yeast with dried yeast, use 1 tablespoon dried yeast for 25 g/1 oz fresh yeast.

Fast-action

Quick-acting yeast – generally now sold as 'fast-action yeast' and also known formerly as 'easy-blend' – cuts down the time of bread-making as it eliminates the need for proving the bread twice and can be added straight to the flour without it needing to be activated. When using quick-acting yeast instead of dried yeast, follow recipes that specifically use fast-action yeast. When using yeast, the most important thing to remember is that yeast is a living plant and needs food, water and warmth to work.

Equipment

Nowadays, you can get lost in the cookware sections of some of the larger stores – they really are a cook's paradise with gadgets, cooking tools and state-of-the-art electronic blenders, mixers and liquidisers. A few well-picked, high-quality utensils and pieces of equipment will be frequently used and will therefore be a much wiser buy than cheaper gadgets.

Cooking equipment not only assists in the kitchen, but can make all the difference between success and failure. Take the humble cake tin: although a very basic piece of cooking equipment, it plays an essential role in baking. Using the incorrect size can mean disaster – a tin that is too large, for example, will spread the mixture too thinly and the result will be a flat, limp-looking cake. On the other hand, cramming the mixture into a tin which is too small will result in the mixture rising up and out of the tin.

Baking Tins & Utensils

To ensure successful baking, it is worth investing in a selection of high-quality tins, which, if looked after properly, should last for many years. Choose heavy-duty metal tins that will not buckle or the new flexible silicone tins – these are easy to turn out, most need very little greasing for a perfect shape and they also wash and dry easily. Follow the manufacturer's instructions when first using and ensure that the tins are thoroughly washed and dried after use and before putting away.

Sandwich Tins

Perhaps the most useful of tins for baking are sandwich tins, ideal for classics such as Victoria sponge, Genoese cake and coffee and walnut cake. You will need two tins, normally 18 cm/7 inches or 20.5 cm/8 inches in diameter and about 5–7.5 cm/2–3 inches deep. They are often nonstick.

Deep Cake Tins

With deep cake tins, it is personal choice whether you buy round or square tins and they vary in size from 12.5–35.5 cm/5–14 inches (a useful size is 20.5 cm/ 8 inches), with a depth of between 12.5–15 cm/5–6 inches. A deep cake tin, for everyday fruit or Madeira cake, is a must.

Loaf Tins

Loaf tins are used for bread, fruit or tea breads and terrines and normally come in two sizes: 450 g/1 lb and 900 g/2 lb.

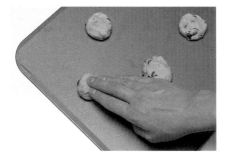

Baking Sheets and Trays

Good baking sheets and trays are a must for all cooks. Dishes that are too hot to handle such as apple pies should be placed directly onto a baking sheet. Meringues, biscuits and cookies are cooked on the sheet. The difference between baking sheets and baking trays – or specific Swiss-roll tins – is that they have sides all around, whereas a sheet only has one raised side, or none.

Other Tins and Dishes

Square or oblong shallow baking tins are also very useful for making traybakes, fudge brownies, flapjacks and shortbread. Then there are patty tins, which are ideal for making small buns, jam tarts or mince pies; and individual Yorkshire pudding tins, muffin tins or flan tins. They are available in a variety of sizes.

There are plenty of other tins to choose from, ranging from themed tins, such as Christmas tree shapes, numbers from 1–9 and tins shaped as petals, to ring-mould tins (tins with a hole in the centre) and springform tins, where the sides release after cooking, allowing the finished cake to be removed easily.

A selection of different-sized roasting tins (deep baking trays) are also a worthwhile investment as they can double up as a *bain-marie*, or for cooking larger quantities of cakes such as gingerbread. A few different tins and dishes are required if baking crumbles, soufflés and pies. Ramekin dishes and small pudding basins can be used for a variety of different recipes, as can small tartlet tins and dariole moulds.

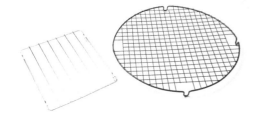

Cooling Racks

Another piece of equipment which is worth having is a wire cooling rack. It is essential when baking to allow biscuits and cakes to cool (in their tins and/or after being removed from their tins), and a wire rack protects your kitchen surfaces from the heat as well as allowing air to circulate around the goodies, speeding cooling and preventing soggy bottoms.

Rolling Pin

When purchasing your implements for baking, perhaps the rolling pin is one of the most important. Ideally, it should be long and thin, and heavy enough to roll the pastry out easily but not too heavy that it is uncomfortable to use. Pastry needs to be rolled out on a flat surface and, although a lightly floured flat surface will do, a marble slab will ensure that the pastry is kept cool and ensures that the fats do not melt while being rolled. This helps to keep the pastry light, crisp and flaky rather than heavy and stodgy, which happens if the fat melts before being baked.

Other Tools

Other useful basic pastry implements are tools such as a pastry brush (which can be used to wet pastry or brush on a glaze), a pastry wheel for cutting and a sieve to remove impurities and also to sift air into the flour, encouraging the pastry or mixture to be lighter in texture.

Basic mixing cutlery is also essential, such as a wooden spoon (for mixing and creaming), a spatula (for transferring the mixture from the mixing bowl to the baking tins and spreading the mixture once it is in the tins) and a palette knife (to ease cakes and breads out of their tins before placing them on the wire racks to cool). Scales and measuring jugs, or measuring spoons and cups, are essential for accurate measuring of both dry and wet ingredients. Three to four different sizes of mixing bowls are also very useful.

Electrical Equipment

Nowadays, help from time-saving gadgets and electrical equipment makes baking far easier and quicker. Equipment can be used for creaming, mixing, beating, whisking, kneading, grating and chopping. There is a wide choice of machines available, from the most basic to the very sophisticated.

Food Processors

When choosing a machine, first, decide what you need your processor to do. If you are a novice to baking, it may be a waste to start with a machine which offers a wide range of implements and functions. This can be off-putting and result in not using the machine to its fullest. In general, while styling and product design play a role in the price, the more you pay, the larger the machine will be with a bigger bowl capacity and many more gadgets attached. Nowadays, you can chop, shred, slice, chip, blend, purée, knead, whisk and cream anything. However, just what basic features should you ensure your machine has before buying it?

When buying a food processor, look for measurements on the side of the processor bowl and machines with a removable feed tube, which allows food or liquid to be added while the motor is still running. Look out for machines that have the facility to increase the capacity of the bowl (ideal when making soup) and have a pulse button for controlled chopping. For many, storage is also an issue, so reversible discs and flex storage, or, on more advanced models, a blade storage compartment or box, can be advantageous.

It is also worth thinking about machines that offer optional extras that can be bought as your cooking requirements change. Mini chopping bowls are available for those wanting to chop small quantities of food. If time is an issue, dishwasher-friendly attachments may be vital. Citrus presses, liquidisers and whisks may all be useful attachments for the individual cook.

Blenders

Blenders often come as attachments to food processors and are generally used for liquidising and puréeing foods. There are two main types of blender. The first is known as a goblet blender. The blades of this blender are at the bottom of the goblet with measurements up the sides. The second blender is portable. It is hand-held and should be placed in a bowl to blend.

Food Mixers

These are ideally suited to mixing cakes and kneading dough, either as a table-top mixer or a hand-held mixer. Both are extremely useful and based on the same principle of mixing or whisking in an open bowl to allow more air to get to the mixture and therefore give a lighter texture.

The table-top mixers are freestanding and are capable of dealing with fairly large quantities of mixture. They are robust machines, capable of easily dealing with kneading dough and heavy cake mixing as well as whipping cream, whisking egg whites or making one-stage cakes. These mixers also offer a wide range of attachments, from liquidisers and juicers, to can openers and mincers.

Hand-held mixers are smaller than freestanding mixers and often come with their own bowl and stand from which they can be lifted off and used as hand-held devices. They have a motorised head with detachable twin whisks. These mixers are particularly versatile as they do not need a specific bowl in which to whisk. Any suitable mixing bowl can be used.

Basic Techniques

There is no mystery to successful baking, it really is easy providing you follow a few simple rules and guidelines. First, read the recipe right through before commencing. There is nothing more annoying than getting to the middle of a recipe and discovering that you are minus one or two of the ingredients. Until you are confident, follow a recipe, do not try a short cut, otherwise you may find that you have left out a vital step which means that the recipe really cannot work. Most of all, have patience, baking is easy – if you can read, you can bake.

Working with Pastry

Pastry dough needs to be kept as cool as possible throughout. Cool hands help, but are not essential. Use cold or iced water, but not too much as pastry does not need to be wet. Make sure that your fat is not runny or melted but firm (this is why block fat is the best). Avoid using too much flour when rolling out as this alters the proportions, and also avoid handling the dough too much. Chill pastry, wrapped in foil or a plastic bag, for 30 minutes after making the dough. Roll in one direction as this helps to ensure that the pastry does not shrink. Allow the pastry to rest, preferably in the refrigerator, after rolling. If you follow these guidelines but still your pastry is not as good as you would like it to be, then make in a processor instead.

Lining a Flan Dish

It is important to choose the right tin or dish to bake with. You will often find that a loose-bottomed metal flan tin is the best option as it conducts heat more efficiently and evenly than a ceramic dish. It also has the added advantage of a removable base, which makes the transfer of the final flan or tart a much simpler process; it simply lifts out, keeping the pastry intact.

Roll the pastry dough out on a lightly floured surface, ensuring that it is a few inches larger than the flan tin. Wrap the pastry round the rolling pin, lift and place in the tin. Carefully ease the pastry into the base and sides of the tin, ensuring that there are no gaps or tears in the pastry. Allow to rest for a few minutes, then trim the edge either with a sharp knife or by rolling a rolling pin across the top of the flan tin. Prick the pastry with the tines of a fork to prevent it from rising up during baking and chill before baking.

Baking Blind

The term 'baking blind' means cooking the pastry case without the filling, resulting in a crisp pastry shell that is either partially or fully cooked, depending on whether the filling needs any cooking. Pastry shells can be prepared ahead of time as they last for several days if stored correctly in an airtight container, or longer if frozen.

To bake blind, line a tin or dish with the prepared pastry dough and allow to rest in the refrigerator for 30 minutes. This will help to minimise shrinkage while it is being cooked. Remove from the refrigerator and lightly prick the base all over with a fork (do not do this if the filling is runny). Simply line the case with a large square of greaseproof paper, big enough to cover both the base and sides of the pastry case. Fill with ceramic baking beans, dried beans or rice. Place on a baking sheet and bake in a preheated oven, generally at 200°C/400°F/Gas Mark 6, remembering that ovens can take at least 15 minutes to reach this heat (unless they are fan/convection ovens, *see* page 25). Cook for 10–12 minutes, then remove from the oven, discarding the paper and beans. Return to the oven and continue to cook for a further 5–10 minutes, depending on whether the filling needs cooking. Normally, unless otherwise stated, individual pastry tartlet cases also benefit from baking blind.

Covering a Pie with a Pastry Lid

To cover a pie, roll out the pastry dough until it is about 5 cm/2 inches larger than the circumference of the dish. Cut a 2.5 cm/1 inch strip from around the outside of the pastry and then moisten the edge of the pie dish you are using. Place the strip on the edge of the dish and brush with water or beaten egg. Generously fill the pie dish until the surface is slightly rounded. Using the rolling pin, lift the remaining pastry and cover the pie dish. Press together, then seal. Using a sharp knife, trim off any excess pastry from around the edges. Try to avoid brushing the edges of the pastry, especially puff pastry, as this prevents the pastry rising evenly. Before placing in the oven, make a small hole in the centre of the pie to allow the steam to escape.

The edges of the pie can be decorated by pressing the back of a fork around the edge of the pie or instead crimp by pinching the edge crust holding the thumb and index finger of one hand against the edge while gently pushing with the index finger of your other hand. Other ways of finishing the pie are to knock up (achieved by gently pressing your index finger down onto the rim and, at the same time, tapping a knife horizontally along the edge, giving it a flaky appearance), or fluting the edges by pressing your thumb down on the edge of the pastry while gently drawing back an all-purpose knife about 1 cm/½ inch and repeating around the rim. Experiment by putting leaves and berries made out of leftover pastry to finish off the pie, then brush the top of the pie with beaten egg.

Greasing and Lining Cake Tins

Most tins will at least need oiling or greasing with butter (butter is better as oil runs off lining paper). If a recipe states that the tin needs lining, do not be tempted to ignore this. Rich fruit cakes and other cakes that take a long time to cook benefit from the tin being lined so that the edges and base do not burn or dry out. Greaseproof paper or baking parchment is ideal for this. It is a good idea to have the paper at least double thickness, or preferably 3–4 thicknesses. Sponge cakes and other cakes that are cooked in 30 minutes or less are also better if the bases are lined as it is far easier to remove them from the tin.

The best way to line a round or square tin is to lightly draw around the base and then cut just inside the markings, making it easy to sit in the tin. Next, lightly grease the paper (with butter) so that it will easily peel away from the cake. If the sides of the tin also need

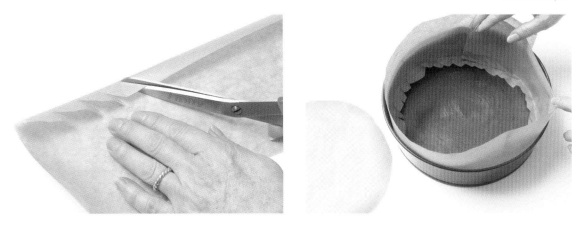

to be lined, then cut a strip of paper long enough for the tin. This can be measured by wrapping a piece of string around the rim of the tin. Once again, lightly grease the paper, push against the tin and grease once more as this will hold the paper to the sides of the tin. Steamed puddings usually need only a disc of greaseproof paper at the bottom of the dish so that it will turn out easily.

Hints for Successful Baking

Measurements

Ensure that the ingredients are accurately measured. A cake that has too much flour or insufficient egg will be dry and crumbly. Take care when measuring the raising agent if used, as too much will mean that the cake will rise too quickly and then sink. Insufficient raising agent means the cake will not rise adequately.

Oven Temperature

Ensure that the oven is preheated to the correct temperature; it can take 10 minutes to reach up to 190°C/375°F/Gas Mark 5, and 15 minutes for above that – but ovens vary. You may find that an oven thermometer is a good investment. Cakes are best if cooked in the centre of the preheated oven. Do try to avoid the temptation of opening the oven door at the beginning of cooking, as a draught of cool air can make the cake sink. *Important:* If using a fan/convection oven, then refer to the manufacturer's instructions, as they normally cook 10–20˚ hotter than conventional ovens and often do not need preheating. As a general rule, preheat your fan oven to 20 per cent lower than is stated for a non-fan oven – this usually works out at 20˚C lower.

Testing to see When a Cake is Cooked

Check that the cake is thoroughly cooked by removing from the oven and inserting a clean skewer into the cake. Leave for 30 seconds and remove. If the skewer is completely clean, then the cake is cooked; if there is a little mixture left on the skewer, then return to the oven for a few minutes.

Problems

Other problems that you may encounter while cake-making are insufficient creaming of the fat and sugar or a curdled creamed mixture (which will result in a densely textured and often fairly solid cake). Flour that has not been folded in carefully enough or has not been mixed with enough raising agent may also result in a fairly heavy consistency. It is very important to try to ensure that the correct size of tin is used, as you may end up either with a flat, hard cake or one which has spilled over the edge of the tin. Another tip to be aware of (especially when cooking with fruit) is that, if the consistency is too soft, the cake will not be able to support the fruit.

Cooling and Storing

Finally, when you take your cake out of the oven, unless the recipe states that it should be left in the tin until cold, leave for a few minutes to settle, then loosen the edges and turn out onto a wire rack to cool. Cakes which are left in the tin for too long will develop a damp, soggy base. When storing, make sure the cake is completely cold before placing it into an airtight tin or plastic container. Generally, biscuits and cakes will keep for about 5 days in an airtight container. However, if a cake uses fresh cream, cream cheese frosting or other fresh ingredients such as fruit, it will only last for 1–2 days kept refrigerated (note: do not refrigerate cakes covered with sugarpaste icing). Cakes with buttercream and similar icings will keep for 2–3 days in a cool place. Light fruit cakes, such as Dundee, will store for about a week and rich fruit cakes such as Christmas Cake will keep for up to 3 months if fortified with alcohol and wrapped tightly in foil.

Basic Recipes: Pastry

Shortcrust Pastry

Makes 225 g/8 oz

225 g/8 oz plain white flour
pinch salt
50 g/2 oz white vegetable fat or lard
50 g/2 oz butter or block margarine

Sift the flour and salt into a mixing bowl. Cut the fats into small pieces and add to the bowl. Rub the fats into the flour using your fingertips until the mixture resembles fine breadcrumbs. Add 1–2 tablespoons of cold water and, using a knife or your hands if easier, mix to form a soft, pliable dough. Knead gently on a lightly floured surface until smooth and free from cracks, then wrap and chill for 30 minutes before rolling out on a lightly floured surface. Use as required. Cook in a preheated hot oven (200°C/400°F/Gas Mark 6).

Sweet Shortcrust Pastry

Makes 225 g/8 oz

225 g/8 oz plain white flour
150 g/5 oz unsalted butter, softened
2 tbsp caster sugar
1 egg yolk

Sift the flour into a mixing bowl, cut the butter into small pieces, add to the bowl and rub into the flour. Stir in the sugar, then mix to form a pliable dough with the egg yolk and about 1 tablespoon of cold water. Wrap, chill for at least 30 minutes or until firm and use as required.

Chocolate Variation

To make sweet chocolate shortcrust pastry, simply sift in 1 tablespoon cocoa powder with the flour after the butter has been rubbed in.

Cheese Pastry

Follow the recipe for sweet shortcrust pastry, but omit the sugar and add 1 teaspoon dried mustard powder and 50 g/2 oz/½ cup mature grated Cheddar cheese.

Rough Puff Pastry

Makes 225 g/8 oz

225 g/8 oz plain flour
pinch salt
150 g/5 oz butter, block margarine or lard
squeeze lemon juice

Sift the flour and salt together in a mixing bowl. Cut up the fat and add to the bowl. Add the lemon juice and 6–7

tablespoons of cold water. Mix with a fork until it is a fairly stiff mixture.

Turn out onto a lightly floured surface. Roll into an oblong. Fold the bottom third up to the centre, bring the top third down to the centre. Gently press the edges together. Give the pastry a half turn, roll the pastry out again into an oblong. Repeat the folding, turning and rolling at least four times. Wrap. Leave to rest in a cool place for at least 30 minutes. Cook as directed by your recipe, in a preheated oven at 220°C/425°F/Gas Mark 7.

Quick Flaky Pastry

125 g/4 oz butter
175 g/6 oz plain flour
pinch salt

Place the butter in the freezer for 30 minutes. Sift the flour and salt into a large bowl. Remove the butter from the freezer and grate using the coarse side of a grater, dipping the butter in the flour every now and again as it makes it easier to grate.

Mix the butter into the flour, using a knife, making sure all the butter is coated thoroughly with flour. Add 2 tablespoons cold water and continue to mix, bringing the mixture together. Use your hands to complete the mixing. Add a little more water if needed to leave a clean bowl. Place the pastry in a polythene bag and chill in the refrigerator for 30 minutes. Cook as directed by your recipe, in a preheated oven at 200°C/400°F/Gas Mark 6.

Choux Pastry

Makes 225 g/8 oz

50 g/2 oz butter
75 g/3 oz plain flour
pinch salt
2 eggs, beaten

Hot Water Crust Pastry

Makes 450 g/1 lb

450 g/1 lb plain flour
1 tsp salt
125 g/4 oz lard or white vegetable fat
150 ml/¼ pt milk and water, mixed

Place the butter and 150 ml/5 fl oz water in a heavy-based saucepan. Heat gently, stirring until the butter has melted, and bring to the boil. Draw off the heat and add the flour and salt all at once. Beat with a wooden spoon until the mixture forms a ball in the centre. Cool for 5 minutes. Gradually add the eggs, beating well after each addition until a stiff mixture is formed. Either place in a piping bag fitted with a large nozzle, or shape using two spoons. Place on a greased baking sheet and bake in a preheated oven at 200˚C/400˚F/Gas Mark 6 for 15–25 minutes, depending on size. Remove and make a small slit in the side, then return to the oven and cook for a further 5 minutes. Remove and cool before filling.

Sift the flour and salt together and reserve. Heat the lard or white vegetable fat until melted. Bring to the boil. Pour immediately into the flour along with some of the milk and water and, using a wooden spoon, mix together and beat until the mixture comes together and forms a ball, using more milk and water as needed. When cool enough to handle, knead lightly until smooth and pliable. Use as required, covering the dough with a clean cloth before use. Bake in a preheated oven at 220˚C/425˚F/Gas Mark 7, or as directed.

Basic Recipes: Batters

Pouring Batter for Yorkshire Puddings and Pancakes

125 g/4 oz plain flour
pinch salt
2 eggs
300 ml/½ pint whole milk and water mixed

Sift the flour and salt into a mixing bowl and make a well in the centre. Drop the eggs into the well with a little milk. Beat the eggs into the flour, gradually drawing the flour in from the sides of the bowl. Once half the milk has been added, beat well until smooth and free from lumps. Stir in the remaining milk and leave to stand for 30 minutes. Stir before using.

Heat 1 tablespoon oil in a roasting tin or individual Yorkshire pudding tins in an oven preheated to 220°C/425°F/Gas Mark 7. When the oil is almost smoking, stir the batter, then pour it into the hot oil. Cook for 30–40 minutes for a large pudding and 18–20 minutes for individual puddings. This batter can also be used for pancakes and, if liked, 2 tbsp caster sugar can be added.

Coating Batter for Fritters

125 g/4 oz plain flour
pinch salt
1 tbsp sunflower oil
150 ml/¼ pint water
2 egg whites

Sift the flour and salt into a mixing bowl and make a well in the centre. Add the oil and half the water and beat until smooth and free from lumps. Gradually beat in the remaining water. Just before using, whisk the egg whites until stiff, then stir into the batter and use immediately.

Basic Recipes: Meringues

Meringue is made from egg whites and caster sugar. As a general rule, allow 1 egg white to 50 g/2 oz caster sugar.

Making Meringue

Place the egg whites in a clean mixing bowl (any grease in the bowl will prevent the egg white from whisking). Use a balloon or wire whisk if whisking by hand, or an electric mixer fitted with a balloon whisk if not. Whisk the egg whites until stiff. To test if they are stiff enough, turn the bowl upside down – if the egg white does not move, it is ready. Slowly add half the sugar, 1 teaspoon at a time, whisking well after each addition. Once half the sugar has been added, add the remaining sugar and gently stir it in with a metal spoon. Take care not to overmix.

Spoon the meringue onto a baking sheet lined with nonstick baking parchment. Shape the meringue according to preference or the recipe – such as in a round 'case' – and bake in a preheated oven at 150˚C/300˚F/Gas Mark 2 for 1½ hours, or until set and firm to the touch. Remove from the oven; leave until cold before using or storing in an airtight container.

Basic Recipes: Icings

Cream Cheese Frosting

Covers 12 small cakes

50 g/2 oz unsalted butter, softened
300 g/11 oz icing sugar, sifted
flavouring of choice
food colourings
125 g/4 oz full-fat cream cheese

Basic Buttercream Frosting

Covers 12 small cakes

150 g/5 oz unsalted butter, softened
225 g/8 oz icing sugar, sifted
2 tbsp hot milk or water
1 tsp vanilla extract
food colourings of choice

Beat the butter and icing sugar together until light and fluffy. Add flavourings and colourings of choice and beat again. Add the cream cheese and whisk until light and fluffy. Do not over-beat, however, as the mixture can become runny.

Beat the butter until light and fluffy, then beat in the sifted icing sugar and hot milk or water in two batches. Add the vanilla extract and any food colourings. Store chilled for up to 2 days in a lidded container.

Variations

Omit the vanilla extract and instead:

Coffee Blend 2 tsp coffee extract with the milk.

Chocolate Blend 2 tbsp cocoa powder to a paste with 2 tbsp boiling water and use instead of the hot milk or water.

Citrus Add the finely grated zest of 1 small orange plus 1 tbsp orange juice or the finely grated zest of 1 lemon or lime and 2 tsp fresh lemon or lime juice instead of the milk or water.

Chocolate Fudge Icing

Covers 12 small cakes

125 g/4 oz dark chocolate, broken into pieces
50 g/2 oz unsalted butter
1 medium egg, beaten
175 g/6 oz natural icing sugar, sifted
½ tsp vanilla extract

Place the chocolate and butter in a bowl over a pan of hot water and stir until melted. Remove from the heat and whisk in the egg with the icing sugar and vanilla. Whisk until smooth and glossy, then use immediately or leave to cool and thicken for a spreading consistency.

Royal Icing

Makes 500 g/1 lb 2 oz to cover 12 deep muffins

2 medium egg whites
500 g/1 lb 2 oz icing sugar, sifted
2 tsp lemon juice

Put the egg whites in a large bowl and whisk lightly with a fork to break up the whites until foamy. Sift in half the icing sugar with the lemon juice and beat well with an electric mixer for 4 minutes or by hand with a wooden spoon for about 10

minutes until smooth. Gradually sift in the remaining icing sugar and beat again until thick, smooth and brilliant white and the icing forms soft peaks when flicked up with a spoon. Keep the royal icing covered with a clean damp cloth until you are ready to use it, or store in the refrigerator in a tightly lidded plastic container until needed. If making royal icing ahead of time to use later, beat it again before use to remove any air bubbles that may have formed in the mixture.

Tip For a softer royal icing that will not set too hard, beat 1 tsp of glycerine into the mixture.

Glacé Icing

Covers 12 small cakes

225 g/8 oz icing sugar
few drops lemon juice or vanilla or almond extract
2–3 tbsp boiling water
liquid food colouring

Sift the icing sugar into a bowl and add the chosen flavouring. Gradually stir in enough water to mix to a consistency of thick cream. Beat with a wooden spoon until the icing is thick enough to coat the back of the spoon. Add colouring if liked and use at once, as the icing will begin to form a skin.

Variations

Citrus Replace the water with freshly squeezed, strained orange or lemon juice.

Chocolate Sift 2 tsp cocoa powder into the icing sugar.

Coffee Dissolve 1 tsp coffee granules in 1 tbsp of the hot water, cool; or add 1 tsp liquid coffee extract.

Apricot Glaze

Makes 450 g/1 lb to cover 24 small cakes

450 g/1 lb apricot jam
3 tbsp water
1 tsp lemon juice

Place the jam, water and juice in a heavy-based saucepan and heat gently, stirring, until soft and melted. Boil rapidly for 1 minute, then press through a fine sieve with the back of a wooden spoon. Discard the pieces of fruit. Use immediately for glazing or sticking on almond paste, or pour into a clean jar or plastic lidded container and store in the refrigerator for up to 3 months.

Almond Paste

Makes 450 g/1 lb to cover 24 small cakes

125 g/4 oz icing sugar, sifted
125 g/4 oz caster sugar
225 g/8 oz ground almonds
1 medium egg
1 tsp lemon juice

Stir the sugars and ground almonds together in a bowl. Whisk the egg and lemon juice together and mix into the dry ingredients. Knead until the paste is smooth. Wrap tightly in clingfilm or foil to keep airtight and store in the refrigerator until needed. The paste can be made 2–3

days ahead of time, but after that it will start to dry out and become difficult to handle. To use the almond paste, knead on a surface lightly dusted with icing sugar until soft and pliable. Brush the top of each cake with apricot glaze. Roll out the almond paste and cut out discs large enough to cover the tops of the cakes. Press onto the cakes.

Sugarpaste Icing

Makes 350 g/12 oz to cover 12 small cakes, or use for decorations

1 medium egg white
1 tbsp liquid glucose
350 g/12 oz icing sugar, sifted

Place the egg white and liquid glucose in a large mixing bowl and stir together with a fork, breaking up the egg white. Add the icing sugar gradually, mixing in with a palette knife until the mixture binds together and forms a ball. Turn the ball of icing out onto a clean surface dusted with icing sugar and

knead for 5 minutes until soft but firm enough to roll out. If the icing is too soft, knead in a little more icing sugar until the mixture is pliable.

To colour, knead in paste food colouring. Do not use liquid food colouring as this is not suitable and will make the sugarpaste go limp.

To use, roll out thinly on a clean surface dusted with icing sugar and cut out a disc large enough to cover the top of each cake. Brush the almond paste (if using as a layer underneath the sugarpaste disc) with a little cold boiled water or a clear spirit such as Kirsch, then press onto the cake, then press the sugarpaste on top of the almond paste topping. Alternatively, coat the cakes with a little buttercream and place the sugarpaste disc on top and press down.

To mould, knead lightly and roll out thinly on a surface dusted with icing sugar. Use cutters or templates to make flat shapes, then mould into 3D shapes with your fingertips and leave to dry out for 24 hours in egg boxes lined with clingfilm.

Culinary Terms Explained

At a glance, here are some of the key terms you will come across when baking. Some we may have discussed already, some may be new to you.

Baking parchment Sometimes called 'silicone-coated paper', 'baking parchment' or 'nonstick baking paper'. Used for wrapping food to be cooked (en papillote) and for lining cake tins to prevent sticking. As it is sold as 'nonstick', this in theory avoids the need to grease or oil the paper.

Greaseproof paper Paper that tends to be relatively nonstick and which is used to line tins for cakes and puddings, but it is advisable to lightly grease this paper to prevent sticking. It is ideal for wrapping food such as packed lunches or fatty foods. Today, greaseproof paper and baking parchment are often able to be used in the same way – check the packaging.

En papillote A French term used to describe food which is baked, but is wrapped in baking parchment before cooking. This works well with fish as the aroma from the different herbs or spices and the fish are contained during cooking and not released until the paper parcel is opened.

Rice paper This edible paper is made from the pith of a Chinese tree and can be used as a base on which to bake delicate or sticky cakes and biscuits such as almond macaroons.

Baking blind The method often used for cooking the pastry case of flans and tarts before the filling is added. After lining the tin with the uncooked pastry, it is then covered with a sheet of greaseproof paper or baking parchment and weighed down with either ceramic baking beans, dried beans or rice and is baked in the oven as directed in the recipe.

Baking powder A raising agent which works by producing carbon dioxide as a consequence of a reaction caused by the acid and alkali ingredients which expand during the baking process and make the breads and cakes rise.

Bicarbonate of soda This alkali powder acts as a raising agent in baking when combined with an acid or acid liquid (cream of tartar, lemon juice, yogurt, buttermilk, cocoa or vinegar, for example).

Cream of tartar An acid raising agent (potassium hydrogen tartrate) often present in both self-raising flour and baking powder. Activates the alkali component of baking powder.

Fermenting A term used during bread-, beer- or wine-making to note the chemical change brought about through the use of a fermenting or leavening agent, such as yeast.

Unleavened Often refers to bread which does not use a raising agent and is therefore flat, such as Indian naan bread.

Cornflour Used to thicken consistency and can also be used in meringue-making to prevent the meringue becoming hard and brittle and to enhance its chewiness.

Curdling When the milk separates from a sauce through acidity or excessive heat. This can also happen to creamed cake mixtures that have separated due to the eggs being too cold or added too quickly.

Sifting The shaking of dry ingredients (primarily flour) through a metal or nylon sieve to remove lumps and impurities, and to add air.

Binding Adding liquid or egg to bring a dry mixture together. Normally, this entails using a fork, spoon or your fingertips.

Blending When two or more ingredients are thoroughly mixed together.

Creaming The method by which fat and sugar are beaten together until lighter in colour and fluffy. By creaming the fat in cake mixtures, air is incorporated into the fairly high fat content. It thus lightens the texture of cakes and puddings.

Folding A method of combining creamed fat and sugar with flour in cake and pudding mixes, usually by carefully mixing with a large metal spoon, either by cutting and folding, or by doing a figure-of-eight in order to maintain a light texture.

Rubbing in The method of combining fat with flour by rubbing them together using your hands. For crumble toppings, shortcrust pastry, biscuits and scones.

Beating The method by which air is introduced into a mixture using a fork, wooden spoon, whisk or electric mixer. Beating is also used as a method to soften ingredients.

Whipping/whisking The term given to incorporating air rapidly into a mixture (either through using a manual whisk or an electric whisk).

Dropping consistency The consistency to which a cake or pudding mixture reaches before being cooked. It tends to be fairly soft (but not runny) and should drop off a spoon in around 5 seconds when tapped lightly on the side of a bowl.

Grinding Reducing hard ingredients, such as nuts, to crumbs, normally by the use of a grinder or a pestle and mortar.

Blender An electric machine with rotating blades used mainly with soft and wet ingredients to purée and liquidise, although it can grind dry ingredients such as nuts and breadcrumbs.

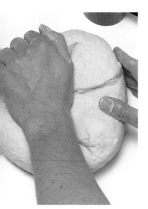

Knead The process of stretching, pummelling and working dough in order to strengthen the gluten in the flour and making the dough more elastic, thus giving a good rise. Also applies to pastry-making; the dough is kneaded on a lightly floured surface to give a smooth and elastic pastry, making it easier to roll and ensuring an even texture after baking. In both cases, the outside of the dough is drawn into the centre.

Proving The term used in bread-making when the bread is allowed to rise a second time after it has been kneaded once and then shaped before it is baked.

Knock back The term used for a second kneading after the dough has been allowed to rise. This is done to ensure an even texture and to disperse any large pockets of air.

Crumb The internal texture of a cake or bread as defined by the air pockets.

En croute Used to describe food which is covered with raw pastry and then baked.

Vol-au-vent Translated, it means to fly or float on the wind. This small and usually round or oval puff pastry case is first baked and then filled with a savoury meat, seafood or vegetable filling in a sauce.

Choux A type of pastry, whose uncooked dough is rather like a glossy batter, which is piped into small balls onto a baking sheet and baked until light and airy. They can then be filled with cream or savoury fillings.

Filo A type of pastry that is wafer thin. Three to four sheets are usually used at a time, buttered, then layered.

Puff pastry Probably the richest of pastries, as it is enriched with a high proportion of butter, which makes a pastry with light flaky layers. When making from the beginning, it requires the lightest of handling.

Brioche A sweet, spongy traditional bread eaten in France for breakfast, often served warm. Brioche is enriched with eggs and butter and has a rich but soft texture, made from a very light yeast dough, and is baked in the shape of a small cottage loaf. A delicious substitute for bread in bread and butter pudding.

Caramel Obtained by heating sugar on a very low heat until it turns liquid and deep brown in colour. This is used in dishes such as crème caramel, which is, in turn, baked in a *bain-marie*.

Bain-marie A French term meaning water bath. A shallow tin, often a roasting tin, is half-filled with water; smaller dishes of food are then placed in it, allowing them to cook at lower temperatures without overheating. This method is often used to cook custards and other egg dishes or to keep some dishes warm.

Ramekin An ovenproof earthenware dish which provides an individual serving.

Cocotte Another name for a ramekin (a small, ovenproof earthenware pot used for individual portions).

Dariole A small narrow mould with sloping sides used for making Madeleines. Darioles can also be used for individual steamed or baked puddings and jellies.

Dusting To sprinkle lightly, often with flour, sugar or icing sugar.

Dredging The sprinkling of food with a coating (generally of flour or sugar). A board may be dredged with flour before the pastry is rolled out and cakes and biscuits can be dredged with sugar or icing sugar after baking.

Glacé A French term meaning glossy or iced. Glacé icing is a quick icing often used to decorate cakes and biscuits. It is made using icing sugar and warm water.

Piping A way in which cakes and desserts are decorated, or the method by which choux pastry is placed onto a baking sheet. This is achieved by putting cream, icing or mixture in a nylon bag (with a nozzle attached), or an improvised piping bag made from a cone of greaseproof paper, and then slowly forcing through the nozzle and piping it onto the cake or baking sheet.

Zest This can refer to the outer, coloured part of an orange, lemon or lime peel, or the very thin, long pieces of that peel. The zest contains the fruit oil, which is responsible for the citrus flavour. Normally, a zester is used to create the strips, as it removes the zest without any of the bitter white pith. Zest can also be grated on a grater into very small pieces, again taking care to only remove the very outer layer.

Useful Conversions

Temperature Conversion

−4°F	−20°C	68°F	20°C
5°F	−15°C	77°F	25°C
14°F	−10°C	86°F	30°C
23°F	−5°C	95°F	35°C
32°F	0°C	104°F	40°C
41°F	5°C	113°F	45°C
50°F	10°C	122°F	50°C
59°F	15°C	212°F	100°C

Oven Temperatures

Bear in mind that, if using a fan oven, you should reduce the stated temperature by around 20°C. Check the manufacturer's instructions for guidance.

110°C	225°F	Gas Mark ¼	Very slow oven
120/130°C	250°F	Gas Mark ½	Very slow oven
140°C	275°F	Gas Mark 1	Slow oven
150°C	300°F	Gas Mark 2	Slow oven
160/170°C	325°F	Gas Mark 3	Moderate oven
180°C	350°F	Gas Mark 4	Moderate oven
190°C	375°F	Gas Mark 5	Moderately hot oven
200°C	400°F	Gas Mark 6	Moderately hot oven
220°C	425°F	Gas Mark 7	Hot oven
230°C	450°F	Gas Mark 8	Hot oven
240°C	475°F	Gas Mark 9	Very hot oven

Dry Weights

Metric/Imperial							
10 g	¼ oz	50 g	2 oz	165 g	5½ oz	300 g	11 oz
15 g	½ oz	65 g	2½ oz	175 g	6 oz	325 g	11½ oz
20 g	¾ oz	75 g	3 oz	185 g	6½ oz	350 g	12 oz
25 g	1 oz	90 g	3½ oz	200 g	7 oz	375 g	13 oz
40 g	1½ oz	100 g	3½ oz	225 g	8 oz	400 g	14 oz
		125 g	4 oz	250 g	9 oz	425 g	15 oz
		150 g	5 oz	275 g	10 oz	450 g	1 lb

Liquid Measures

Metric, Imperial (UK) and US Cups/Quarts

2.5 ml	½ tsp	-	-
5 ml	1 tsp	-	-
15 ml	1 tbsp	-	-
25 ml	1 fl oz	⅛ cup	2 tbsp
50 ml	2 fl oz	¼ cup	3–4 tbsp
65 ml	2½ fl oz	⅓ cup	5 tbsp
75–85 ml	3 fl oz	⅓ cup	6 tbsp
100 ml	3½ fl oz	⅓ cup	7 tbsp
125 ml	4 fl oz	½ cup	8 tbsp
135 ml	4½ fl oz	½ cup	9 tbsp
150 ml	5 fl oz	¼ pint	⅔ cup
175 ml	6 fl oz	⅓ pint	scant ¾ cup
200 ml	7 fl oz	⅓ pint	¾ cup
225 ml	8 fl oz	⅜ pint	1 cup
240 ml	8 fl oz	⅜ pint	1 cup
250 ml	8 fl oz	⅜ pint	1 cup
275 ml	9 fl oz	½ pint	1⅛ cups
300 ml	10 fl oz	½ pint	1¼ cups
350 ml	12 fl oz	⅔ pint	1½ cups
400 ml	14 fl oz	⅝ pint	1⅔ cups
450 ml	15 fl oz	¾ pint	1¾ cups
475 ml	16 fl oz	⅞ pint	2 scant cups
500 ml	18 fl oz	⅞ pint	2 cups
600 ml	20 fl oz	1 pint	2½ cups
750 ml	26 fl oz	1¼ pints	3¼ cups
900 ml	-	1½ pints	1 scant quart
1 litre	-	1¾ pints	1 quart
1.1 litres	-	2 pints	1¼ quarts
1.2 litres	-	2 pints	1¼ quarts
1.25 litres	-	2¼ pints	1⅓ quarts
1.3 litres	-	2⅓ pints	1⅓ quarts
1.4 litres	-	2½ pints	1½ quarts
1.5 litres	-	2½ pints	1⅔ quarts
1.6 litres	-	2¾ pints	1¾ quarts
1.7 litres	-	3 pints	1¾ quarts
1.8 litres	-	3⅛ pints	1⅞ quarts
1.9 litres	-	3⅓ pints	2 quarts
2 litres	-	3½ pints	2 quarts
2.25 litres	-	4 pints	2⅜ quarts
2.5 litres	-	4½ pints	2⅔ quarts
2.75 litres	-	5 pints	3 quarts

Classic Ca...
& Bakes

Baking for Beginners

SERVES 8

Easy Victoria Sponge

225 g/8 oz soft margarine
225 g/8 oz caster sugar
4 medium eggs
1 tsp vanilla extract

225 g/8 oz self-raising flour
1 tsp baking powder
icing sugar, to dust

For the filling:
4 tbsp seedless raspberry jam
100 ml/3½ fl oz double cream

Preheat the oven to 180°C/350°F/Gas Mark 4. Grease two 20.5 cm/8 inch sandwich tins and line the bases with nonstick baking parchment.

Place the margarine, sugar, eggs and vanilla extract in a large bowl and sift in the flour and baking powder. Beat for about 2 minutes until smooth and blended, then divide between the tins and smooth level.

Bake for about 25 minutes until golden, well risen and the tops of the cakes spring back when lightly touched with a fingertip. Leave to cool in the tins for 2 minutes, then turn out onto a wire rack to cool. When cold, peel away the baking parchment.

When completely cold, spread one cake with jam and place on a serving plate. Whip the cream until it forms soft peaks, then spread on the underside of the other cake. Sandwich the two cakes together and sift a little icing sugar over the top.

Fat–free Sponge

SERVES 8

3 medium eggs
175 g/6 oz caster sugar, plus
    extra for dusting
125 g/4 oz self-raising flour,
    plus extra for dusting

To decorate:
150 ml/¼ pint low-fat
    whipping cream, or low-fat
    crème fraiche or yogurt
2 tbsp lemon curd

125 g/4 oz blueberries
zest of 1 lemon, cut into long
    thin strips

Preheat the oven to 190°C/375°F/Gas Mark 5. Grease two nonstick 18 cm/7 inch sandwich tins, line with nonstick baking parchment, then dust with a mixture of flour and caster sugar.

Put the eggs and sugar in a large bowl and stand this over a pan of hot water. Whisk the eggs and sugar until doubled in volume and the mixture is thick enough to leave a trail on the surface of the batter when the whisk is lifted away.

Remove the bowl from the heat and continue whisking for a further 5 minutes until the mixture is cool. Sift half the flour over the mixture and fold in very lightly, using a large metal spoon. Sift in the remaining flour and fold in the same way.

Pour the mixture into the prepared tins and tilt them to spread the mixture evenly. Bake for 15–20 minutes until well risen and firm and the cakes are beginning to shrink away from the sides of the tins. Leave to stand for 2 minutes, then turn out to cool on a wire rack.

To decorate, whip the cream, if using, and spread half the cream (or crème fraîche or yogurt) over one cake. Swirl 1 tablespoon lemon curd into the cream, crème fraîche or yogurt and scatter over half the blueberries. Place the other cake on top and swirl over the remaining cream/yogurt. Swirl over 1 tablespoon lemon curd and sprinkle with the remaining berries. Scatter the strips of lemon zest over the top.

Carrot Cake

CUTS INTO 8 SLICES

200 g/7 oz plain flour
½ tsp ground cinnamon
½ tsp freshly grated nutmeg
1 tsp baking powder
1 tsp bicarbonate of soda
150 g/5 oz dark
    muscovado sugar
200 ml/7 fl oz vegetable oil

3 medium eggs
225 g/8 oz carrots, peeled
    and roughly grated
50 g/2 oz chopped walnuts

For the icing:
175 g/6 oz cream cheese
finely grated zest of 1 orange

1 tbsp orange juice
1 tsp vanilla extract
125 g/4 oz icing sugar

Preheat the oven to 150°C/300°F/Gas Mark 2, 10 minutes before baking. Lightly oil and line the base of a 15 cm/ 6 inch deep square cake tin with greaseproof or baking paper.

Sift the flour, spices, baking powder and bicarbonate of soda together into a large bowl. Stir in the dark muscovado sugar and mix together.

Lightly whisk the oil and eggs together, then gradually stir into the flour and sugar mixture. Stir well. Add the carrots and walnuts. Mix thoroughly, then pour into the prepared cake tin. Bake in the preheated oven for 1¼ hours, or until light and springy to the touch and a skewer inserted into the centre of the cake comes out clean.

Remove from the oven and allow to cool in the tin for 5 minutes before turning out onto a wire rack. Reserve until cold.

To make the icing, beat together the cream cheese, orange zest, orange juice and vanilla extract. Sift the icing sugar and stir into the cream cheese mixture.

When the cake is cold, discard the lining paper, spread the cream cheese icing over the top and serve cut into squares.

Banana Cake

3 medium-sized ripe bananas	250 g/9 oz self-raising flour	1 tsp each ground cinnamon
1 tsp lemon juice	1 tsp ground cinnamon	and caster sugar,
150 g/5 oz soft brown sugar	3 medium eggs	to decorate
75 g/3 oz butter or margarine	50 g/2 oz walnuts, chopped	fresh cream, to serve

Preheat the oven to 190°C/375°F/Gas Mark 5, 10 minutes before baking. Lightly oil and line the base of an 18 cm/7 inch deep round cake tin with greaseproof or baking paper.

Mash 2 of the bananas in a small bowl, sprinkle with the lemon juice and a heaped tablespoon of the sugar. Mix together lightly and reserve.

Gently heat the remaining sugar and butter or margarine in a small saucepan until the butter has just melted.

Pour into a small bowl, then allow to cool slightly. Sift the flour and cinnamon into a large bowl and make a well in the centre.

Beat the eggs into the cooled sugar mixture, pour into the well of flour and mix thoroughly.

Gently stir in the mashed banana mixture. Pour half of the mixture into the prepared tin. Thinly slice the remaining banana and arrange over the cake mixture.

Sprinkle over the chopped walnuts, then cover with the remaining cake mixture.

Bake in the preheated oven for 50–55 minutes until well risen and golden brown. Allow to cool in the tin, turn out and sprinkle with the ground cinnamon and caster sugar. Serve hot or cold with a jug of fresh cream for pouring.

Fruit Cake

225 g/8 oz butter or
  margarine
200 g/7 oz soft brown sugar
finely grated zest of 1 orange
1 tbsp black treacle
3 large eggs, beaten

275 g/10 oz plain flour
¼ tsp ground cinnamon
½ tsp mixed spice
pinch freshly
  grated nutmeg
¼ tsp bicarbonate of soda

75 g/3 oz mixed peel
50 g/2 oz glacé cherries
125 g/4 oz raisins
125 g/4 oz sultanas
125 g/4 oz ready-to-eat dried
  apricots, chopped

Preheat the oven to 150°C/300°F/Gas Mark 2, 10 minutes before baking. Lightly oil and line a 23 cm/9 inch deep round cake tin with a double thickness of greaseproof paper.

In a large bowl, cream together the butter or margarine, sugar and orange zest, until light and fluffy, then beat in the treacle. Beat in the eggs a little at a time, beating well between each addition.

Reserve 1 tablespoon of the flour. Sift the remaining flour, the spices and bicarbonate of soda into the mixture.

Mix all the fruits and the reserved flour together, then stir into the cake mixture. Turn into the prepared tin and smooth the top, making a small hollow in the centre of the cake mixture. Bake in the preheated oven for 1 hour, then reduce the heat to 140°C/275°F/Gas Mark 1.

Bake for a further 1½ hours, or until cooked and a skewer inserted into the centre comes out clean. Leave to cool in the tin, then turn the cake out and serve.

Dundee Cake

400 g/14 oz mixed dried fruit
50 g/2 oz ground almonds
finely grated zest and juice
    of 1 lemon

150 g/5 oz butter, at
    room temperature
150 g/5 oz natural golden
    caster sugar

3 medium eggs, beaten
125 g/4 oz plain flour
40 g/1½ oz whole
    blanched almonds

Preheat the oven to 180°C/350°F/Gas Mark 4. Grease and line the base of an 18 cm/7 inch deep round cake tin with nonstick baking parchment.

Place the dried fruits in a bowl and stir in the ground almonds to coat the dried fruit.

Grate the zest finely from the lemon into the bowl, then squeeze out 1 tablespoon of juice and add to the same bowl. In another bowl, beat the butter and sugar together until light and fluffy. Whisk in the eggs a little at a time, adding 1 teaspoon of flour with each addition.

Sift in the remaining flour, then add the fruit and almond mixture. Fold together with a large metal spoon until smooth. Spoon the mixture into the tin and make a dip in the centre with the back of a spoon. Arrange the almonds over the top in circles.

Bake for 1 hour, then reduce the heat to 150°C/300°F/Gas Mark 2 and bake for a further, hour or until a skewer inserted into the centre comes out clean. Cool in the tin for 5 minutes, then turn out to cool on a wire rack.

Christmas Cake

SERVES 12–14

900 g/2 lb mixed dried fruit
75 g/3 oz glacé cherries,
   rinsed and halved
3 tbsp brandy or orange juice
finely grated zest and juice
   of 1 lemon
225 g/8 oz soft dark
   muscovado sugar

225 g/8 oz butter, at room
   temperature
4 medium eggs, beaten
225 g/8 oz plain flour
1 tbsp black treacle
1 tbsp mixed spice

To decorate:
2–4 tbsp brandy (optional)
4 tbsp sieved apricot jam
700 g/1½ lb almond paste
1 kg/ 2 lb 3 oz ready-to-roll
   sugarpaste
icing sugar, for dusting
bought decorations and ribbon

Place the mixed dried fruit and cherries in a bowl and sprinkle over the brandy or orange juice and the lemon zest and juice. Stir and leave to soak for 2–4 hours. Preheat the oven to 150°C/300°F/Gas Mark 2. Grease and double line the base and sides of a 20.5 cm/8 inch round deep cake tin. Beat the sugar and butter together until soft and fluffy. Beat the eggs in gradually, adding 1 teaspoon flour with each addition. Stir in the treacle, then sift in the rest of the flour and the spice. Add the soaked fruit and stir until the mixture is smooth. Spoon into the tin and smooth the top level. Bake for 1 hour, then reduce the temperature to 140°C/275°F/Gas Mark 1 and bake for a further 2–2½ hours until a skewer inserted into the centre comes out clean. Leave the cake to cool in the tin, then, when completely cold, remove from the tin, wrap in greaseproof paper and then in foil and store in a cool place for 1–3 months.

To decorate, brush the cake all over with brandy, if using. Heat the jam and brush over the top and sides. Roll out one third of the almond paste and cut into a disc the size of the top of the cake using the empty tin as a guide. Place the disc on top. Roll the remaining paste into a strip long enough to cover the sides of the cake and press on. Leave the almond paste to dry out for 2 days in a cool place. On a surface dusted with icing sugar, roll out the sugarpaste to a circle large enough to cover the top and sides of the cake. Brush 1 tablespoon brandy, or cold boiled water, over the almond paste and place the sugarpaste on top. Smooth down and trim. Make a border from tiny balls of sugarpaste and decorate.

Lemon Drizzle Cake

**CUTS INTO
16 SLICES**

125 g/4 oz butter or
   margarine
175 g/6 oz caster sugar
2 large eggs

175 g/6 oz self-raising flour
2 lemons, preferably
   unwaxed
50 g/2 oz granulated sugar

Preheat the oven to 180°C/350°F/Gas Mark 4, 10 minutes before baking. Lightly oil and line the base of an 18 cm/7 inch square cake tin with baking paper.

In a large bowl, cream the butter or margarine and sugar together until soft and fluffy.

Beat the eggs, then gradually add a little of the egg to the creamed mixture, adding 1 tablespoon of flour after each addition.

Finely grate the zest from 1 of the lemons and stir into the creamed mixture, beating well until smooth. Squeeze the juice from the lemon, strain, then stir into the mixture. Spoon into the prepared tin, level the surface and bake in the preheated oven for 25–30 minutes. Using a zester, remove the peel from the last lemon and mix with 25 g/1 oz of the granulated sugar and reserve.

Squeeze the juice into a small saucepan. Add the rest of the granulated sugar to the lemon juice in the saucepan and heat gently, stirring occasionally. When the sugar has dissolved, simmer gently for 3–4 minutes until syrupy.

With a cocktail stick or fine skewer, prick the cake all over. Sprinkle the lemon zest and sugar over the top of the cake, drizzle over the syrup and leave to cool in the tin. Cut the cake into squares and serve.

Orange Fruit Cake

For the orange cake:
225 g/8 oz self-raising flour
2 tsp baking powder
225 g/8 oz caster sugar
225 g/8 oz butter, softened
4 large eggs
grated zest of 1 orange
2 tbsp orange juice
2–3 tbsp Cointreau

125 g/4 oz chopped nuts
Cape gooseberries,
   blueberries, raspberries
   and mint sprigs,
   to decorate
icing sugar, to dust (optional)

For the filling:
450 ml/¾ pint double cream

50 ml/2 fl oz Greek yogurt
½ tsp vanilla extract
2–3 tbsp Cointreau
1 tbsp icing sugar
450 g/1 lb orange fruits, such
   as mango, peach,
   nectarine, papaya and
   yellow plums

(This recipe will test your skills a little more.) Preheat the oven to 180°C/350°F/Gas Mark 4, 10 minutes before baking. Lightly oil and line the base of a 25.5 cm/10 inch deep cake tin or springform tin with nonstick baking parchment.

Sift the flour and baking powder into a large bowl and stir in the sugar. Make a well in the centre and add the butter, eggs, grated zest and orange juice. Beat until blended and a smooth batter is formed. Turn into the tin and smooth the top. Bake in the preheated oven for 35–45 minutes until golden and the sides begin to shrink from the edge of the tin. Remove and cool before removing from the tin and discarding the lining paper.

Using a serrated knife, slice off the top third of the cake, cutting horizontally. Sprinkle the cut sides with the Cointreau. For the filling, whip the cream and yogurt with the vanilla extract, Cointreau and icing sugar until soft peaks form. Chop the orange fruit and fold into the cream. Spread some of this mixture onto the bottom cake layer. Transfer to a serving plate. Cover with the top layer of sponge and spread the remaining cream mixture over the top and sides.

Press the chopped nuts into the sides of the cake and decorate the top with the berries and mint sprigs. If liked, dust the top with icing sugar and serve.

Toffee Apple Cake

CUTS INTO 8 SLICES

2 small eating apples, peeled
4 tbsp soft dark brown sugar
175 g/6 oz butter or
    margarine

175 g/6 oz caster sugar
3 medium eggs
175 g/6 oz self-raising flour
150 ml/¼ pint double cream

2 tbsp icing sugar
½ tsp vanilla extract
½ tsp ground cinnamon

Preheat the oven to 180°C/350°F/Gas Mark 4, 10 minutes before baking time. Lightly oil and line the bases of 2 x 20.5 cm/8 inch sandwich tins with greaseproof or baking paper.

Thinly slice the apples and toss in the brown sugar until well coated. Arrange them over the bases of the prepared tins and reserve.

Cream together the butter or margarine and caster sugar until light and fluffy.

Beat the eggs together in a small bowl and gradually beat them into the creamed mixture, beating well between each addition. Sift the flour into the mixture and, using a metal spoon or rubber spatula, fold in.

Divide the mixture between the two cake tins and level the surface. Bake in the preheated oven for 25–30 minutes until golden and well risen. Leave in the tins to cool.

Lightly whip the cream with 1 tablespoon of the icing sugar and the vanilla extract. Sandwich the cakes together with the cream. Mix the remaining icing sugar and the ground cinnamon together, sift over the top of the cake and serve.

Honey Cake

CUTS INTO
6 SLICES

50 g/2 oz butter
25 g/1 oz caster sugar
125 g/4 oz clear honey
175 g/6 oz plain flour

½ tsp bicarbonate of soda
½ tsp mixed spice
1 medium egg
2 tbsp milk

25 g/1 oz flaked almonds
1 tbsp clear honey,
   to drizzle

Preheat the oven to 180°C/350°F/Gas Mark 4, 10 minutes before baking. Lightly oil and line the base of an 18 cm/7 inch deep round cake tin with lightly oiled greaseproof or baking parchment.

In a saucepan, gently heat the butter, sugar and honey until the butter has just melted.

Sift the flour, bicarbonate of soda and mixed spice together into a bowl.

Beat the egg and the milk until mixed thoroughly.

Make a well in the centre of the sifted flour and pour in the melted butter and honey. Using a wooden spoon, beat well, gradually drawing in the flour from the sides of the bowl. When all the flour has been beaten in, add the egg mixture and mix thoroughly. Pour into the prepared tin and sprinkle with the flaked almonds.

Bake in the preheated oven for 30–35 minutes until well risen and golden brown and a skewer inserted into the centre of the cake comes out clean.

Remove from the oven and cool for a few minutes in the tin before turning out and leaving to cool on a wire rack. Drizzle with the remaining tablespoon of honey and serve.

Almond Cake

CUTS INTO 8 SLICES

225 g/8 oz butter or
  margarine
225 g/8 oz caster sugar
3 large eggs

1 tsp vanilla extract
1 tsp almond extract
125 g/4 oz self-raising flour
175 g/6 oz ground almonds

50 g/2 oz whole almonds,
  blanched
25 g/1 oz dark chocolate

Preheat the oven to 150°C/300°F/Gas Mark 2. Lightly oil and line the base of a 20.5 cm/8 inch deep round cake tin with greaseproof or baking paper.

Cream together the butter or margarine and sugar with a wooden spoon until light and fluffy.

Beat the eggs and extracts together. Gradually add to the sugar and butter mixture and mix well between each addition.

Sift the flour and mix with the ground almonds. Beat into the egg mixture until well mixed and smooth. Pour into the prepared cake tin.

Roughly chop the whole almonds and scatter over the cake. Bake in the preheated oven for 45 minutes, or until golden and risen and a skewer inserted into the centre of the cake comes out clean. Remove from the tin and leave to cool on a wire rack.

Melt the chocolate in a small bowl placed over a saucepan of gently simmering water, stirring until smooth and free of lumps. Drizzle the melted chocolate over the cooled cake and serve once the chocolate has set.

Gingerbread

CUTS INTO 8 SLICES

175 g/6 oz butter or
  margarine
225 g/8 oz black treacle
50 g/2 oz dark
  muscovado sugar

350 g/12 oz plain flour
2 tsp ground ginger
150 ml/¼ pint milk, warmed
2 medium eggs
1 tsp bicarbonate of soda

1 piece stem ginger
  in syrup
1 tbsp stem ginger syrup

Preheat the oven to 150°C/300°F/Gas Mark 2, 10 minutes before baking. Lightly oil and line the base of a 20.5 cm/8 inch deep round cake tin with greaseproof or baking paper.

In a saucepan, gently heat the butter or margarine, black treacle and sugar, stirring occasionally, until the butter melts. Leave to cool slightly.

Sift the flour and ground ginger into a large bowl. Make a well in the centre, then pour in the treacle mixture. Reserve 1 tablespoon of the milk, then pour the rest into the treacle mixture. Stir together lightly until mixed.

Beat the eggs together, then stir into the mixture.

Dissolve the bicarbonate of soda in the remaining 1 tablespoon of warmed milk and add to the mixture. Beat the mixture until well mixed and free of lumps. Pour into the prepared tin and bake in the preheated oven for 1 hour, or until well risen and a skewer inserted into the centre comes out clean.

Cool in the tin, then remove. Slice the stem ginger into thin slivers and sprinkle over the cake. Drizzle with the syrup and serve.

Drop Scones

MAKES 18 SCONES

white vegetable fat,
  for greasing
175 g/6 oz self-raising flour
1 tsp baking powder

40 g/1½ oz caster sugar
1 medium egg
200 ml/7 fl oz milk
butter and syrup, to serve

Grease a heavy-based nonstick frying pan or a flat griddle pan with white vegetable fat and heat gently.

Sift the flour and baking powder into a bowl, stir in the sugar and make a well in the centre. Add the egg and half the milk and beat to a smooth thick batter. Beat in enough of the remaining milk to give the consistency of thick cream.

Drop the mixture onto the hot pan 1 heaped tablespoon at a time, spacing them well apart. When small bubbles rise to the surface of each scone, flip them over with a palette knife and cook for about 1 minute until golden brown.

Place on a serving dish and keep warm, covered with a clean cloth, while you cook the remaining mixture. Serve warm with butter and syrup and eat on the day of making.

Easy Danish Pastries

MAKES 16

500 g/1 lb 2 oz strong
   white flour
½ tsp salt
350 g/12 oz butter
7 g sachet fast-action yeast
50 g/2 oz caster sugar

150 ml/¼ pint lukewarm milk
2 medium eggs, beaten

For the filling and topping:
225 g/8 oz almond paste,
   grated (*see* page 34)

8 canned apricot
   halves, drained
1 egg, beaten
125 g/4 oz fondant icing sugar
50 g/2 oz glacé cherries
50 g/2 oz flaked almonds

Sift the flour and salt into a bowl, add 50 g/2 oz of the butter and rub in until the mixture resembles fine crumbs, then stir in the yeast and sugar. Stir in the milk and beaten eggs and mix to a soft dough. Knead by hand for 10 minutes until smooth or place in a tabletop mixer fitted with a dough hook and knead for 5 minutes. Cover with oiled clingfilm and leave for about 1 hour in a warm place or until doubled in size. Place the dough on a floured surface and knead to knock out the air for about 4 minutes until smooth. Roll out into a rectangle 20 x 35 cm/8 x 14 inches. Dot two thirds of the dough with half the remaining butter, leaving one third plain. Fold the plain third up over the buttered section, then fold the top third over this to form a square parcel. Press the edges to seal, then turn the dough, with the fold to the left. Roll out again to a rectangle and dot with the remaining butter as before. Chill for 15 minutes, then roll out and fold again. Roll, fold and chill once more.

Preheat the oven to 220°C/425°F/Gas Mark 7. Roll out the dough into a 55 cm/22 inch square and cut into 16 squares. Put 25 g/1 oz of the grated almond paste in the centre of each. Take eight of the squares and cut the corners almost to the middle and fold over the alternate points. Top each of the remaining squares with an apricot half and fold the opposite corners over to cover the apricots. Arrange all the pastries on buttered baking sheets and leave to rise for 20 minutes until puffy. Brush with beaten egg and bake for 15 minutes until golden. When cold, mix the fondant icing sugar with enough water to make a smooth icing. Drizzle over the pastries and place a halved cherry on the windmill shapes. Scatter the apricot-filled pastries with flaked almonds and leave to set for 30 minutes.

Jammy Buns

MAKES 12

175 g/6 oz plain flour
175 g/6 oz wholemeal flour
2 tsp baking powder
150 g/5 oz butter or
    margarine

125 g/4 oz golden
    caster sugar
50 g/2 oz dried cranberries
1 large egg, beaten
1 tbsp milk

4–5 tbsp seedless
    raspberry jam

Preheat the oven to 190°C/375°F/Gas Mark 5, 10 minutes before baking. Lightly oil a large baking sheet.

Sift the flours and baking powder together into a large bowl, then tip in the grains remaining in the sieve.

Cut the butter or margarine into small pieces. (It is easier to do this when the butter is in the flour, as it helps stop the butter from sticking to the knife.) Rub the butter into the flours until it resembles coarse breadcrumbs. Stir in the sugar and cranberries.

Using a round-bladed knife, stir in the beaten egg and milk. Mix to form a firm dough. Divide the mixture into 12 and roll into balls.

Place the dough balls on the baking tray, leaving enough space for expansion. Press the thumb into the centre of each ball, making a small hollow. Spoon a little of the jam in each hollow. Brush the top of the buns lightly with milk. Bake in the preheated oven for 20–25 minutes until golden brown. Cool on a wire rack and serve.

Chestnut Cake

SERVES 8-10

175 g/6 oz butter, softened
175 g/6 oz caster sugar
250 g can sweetened
    chestnut purée
3 medium eggs,
    lightly beaten

175 g/6 oz plain flour
1 tsp baking powder
pinch ground cloves
1 tsp fennel seeds, crushed
75 g/3 oz raisins
50 g/2 oz pine nuts, toasted

125 g/4 oz icing sugar
5 tbsp lemon juice
pared strips lemon zest,
    to decorate

Preheat the oven to 150°C/300°F/Gas Mark 2. Oil and line a 23 cm/9 inch springform tin. Beat together the butter and sugar until light and fluffy. Add the chestnut purée and beat. Gradually add the eggs, beating after each addition. Sift in the flour with the baking powder and cloves. Add the fennel seeds and beat. The mixture should drop easily from a wooden spoon when tapped against the side of the bowl. If not, add a little milk.

Beat in the raisins and pine nuts. Spoon the mixture into the prepared tin and smooth the top. Transfer to the centre of the oven and bake in the preheated oven for 55–60 minutes until a skewer inserted in the centre of the cake comes out clean. Remove from the oven and leave in the tin.

Meanwhile, mix together the icing sugar and lemon juice in a small saucepan until smooth. Heat gently until hot, but not boiling. Using a cocktail stick or skewer, poke holes all over the cake. Pour the hot syrup evenly over the cake and leave to soak into the cake. Decorate with pared strips of lemon and serve.

Crispy Rice Cakes

MAKES 18–20

75 g/3 oz butter
150 g/5 oz mini
   marshmallows
75 g/3 oz milk chocolate

50 g/2 oz dried, ready-to-eat
   apricots, finely chopped
25 g/1 oz glacé cherries,
   finely chopped

125 g/4 oz puffed rice
   breakfast cereal

Place 20 paper fairy-cake cases in two 12-hole bun trays.

Put the butter and marshmallows in a heavy-based saucepan and add the chocolate broken into pieces. Melt together very gently over a low heat, stirring the mixture, until melted and sticky.

Remove from the heat and add the chopped apricots and cherries. Add the cereal and stir together with a large metal spoon.

While it is still warm, spoon the mixture into the paper cases and leave to set in the refrigerator for 30 minutes. Eat on the day of making.

Easy Chocolate Cake

SERVES 8–10

75 g/3 oz dark chocolate,
   broken into squares
200 ml/7 fl oz milk
250 g/9 oz dark
   muscovado sugar
75 g/3 oz butter, softened
2 medium eggs, beaten

150 g/5 oz plain flour
½ tsp vanilla extract
1 tsp bicarbonate of soda
25 g/1 oz cocoa powder

For the topping and filling:
125 g/4 oz unsalted butter

225 g/8 oz icing sugar, sifted
175 g/6 oz fresh
   strawberries, halved
tiny mint sprigs, to decorate

Preheat the oven to 180°C/350°F/Gas Mark 4. Grease two 20.5 cm/8 inch round sandwich tins and line the bases with nonstick baking parchment. Place the chocolate, milk and 75 g/3 oz of the sugar in a heavy-based saucepan. Heat gently until the mixture has melted, then set aside to cool.

Place the butter and remaining sugar in a large bowl and whisk with an electric mixer until light and fluffy. Gradually whisk in the eggs, adding 1 teaspoon flour with each addition. Stir in the cooled melted chocolate mixture along with the vanilla extract. Sift in the flour, bicarbonate of soda and cocoa powder, then fold into the mixture until smooth.

Spoon the batter into the tins and smooth level. Bake for about 30 minutes until a skewer inserted in the centre comes out clean. Turn out to cool on a wire rack.

To decorate, beat the butter with the icing sugar and 1 tablespoon warm water until light and fluffy, then place half in a piping bag fitted with a star nozzle. Spread half the buttercream over one sponge layer and scatter half the strawberries over it. Top with the other cake and spread the remaining buttercream over the top. Pipe a border of stars around the edge. Decorate with the remaining strawberries and mint sprigs.

Marble Cake

225 g/8 oz butter
or margarine
225 g/8 oz caster sugar
4 medium eggs
225 g/8 oz self-raising
flour, sifted

finely grated rind and
juice of 1 orange
25 g/1 oz cocoa
powder, sifted

For the topping:
zest and juice of 1 orange
1 tbsp granulated sugar

Preheat the oven to 190°C/375°F/Gas Mark 5, 10 minutes before baking. Lightly oil and line the base of a 20.5 cm/8 inch deep round cake tin with greaseproof or baking paper. In a large bowl, cream the butter or margarine and sugar together until light and fluffy.

Beat the eggs together. Beat into the creamed mixture a little at a time, beating well between each addition. When all the egg has been added, fold in the flour with a metal spoon or rubber spatula.

Divide the mixture equally between two bowls. Beat the grated orange zest into one of the bowls with a little of the orange juice. Mix the cocoa powder with the remaining orange juice until smooth, then add to the other bowl and beat well. Spoon the mixture into the prepared tin, in alternate spoonfuls. When all the cake mixture is in the tin, take a skewer and swirl it in the two mixtures. Tap the base of the tin on the work surface to level the mixture. Bake in the preheated oven for 50 minutes, or until cooked and a skewer inserted into the centre of the cake comes out clean. Remove from the oven and leave in the tin for a few minutes before cooling on a wire rack. Discard the lining paper.

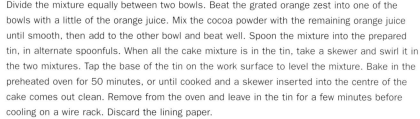

For the topping, place the orange zest and juice with the granulated sugar in a small saucepan and heat gently until the sugar has dissolved. Bring to the boil and simmer gently for 3–4 minutes until the juice is syrupy. Pour over the cooled cake and serve when cool.

Coffee & Pecan Cake

175 g/6 oz self-raising flour
125 g/4 oz butter or
    margarine
175 g/6 oz golden
    caster sugar
1 tbsp instant coffee powder
    or granules

2 large eggs
50 g/2 oz pecans,
    roughly chopped

For the icing:
75 g/3 oz unsalted
    butter, softened

175 g/6 oz icing sugar, sifted
1 tsp instant coffee powder
    or granules
1 tsp cocoa powder
whole pecans, to decorate

Preheat the oven to 190°C/375°F/Gas Mark 5, 10 minutes before baking. Lightly oil and line the bases of two 18 cm/7 inch sandwich tins with greaseproof or baking paper. Sift the flour and reserve.

Beat the butter or margarine and sugar together until light and creamy. Dissolve the coffee in 2 tablespoons hot water and allow to cool.

Lightly mix the eggs with the coffee liquid. Gradually beat into the creamed butter and sugar, adding a little of the sifted flour with each addition.

Fold in the pecans, then divide the mixture between the prepared tins and bake in the preheated oven for 20–25 minutes until well risen and firm to the touch. Leave to cool in the tins for 5 minutes before turning out and cooling on a wire rack.

To make the icing, beat together the butter and icing sugar. Then blend together the coffee and cocoa powder with enough boiling water to make a stiff paste. Beat into the butter and icing sugar.

Sandwich the 2 cakes together using half of the icing. Spread the remaining icing over the top of the cake and decorate with the whole pecans to serve.

Chocolate Pecan Traybake

175 g/6 oz butter
75 g/3 oz icing sugar, sifted
175 g/6 oz plain flour
25 g/1 oz self-raising flour
25 g/1 oz cocoa powder

For the pecan topping:
75 g/3 oz butter
50 g/2 oz light
    muscovado sugar
2 tbsp golden syrup

2 tbsp milk
1 tsp vanilla extract
2 medium eggs,
    lightly beaten
125 g/4 oz pecan halves

Preheat the oven to 180°C/350°F/Gas Mark 4, 10 minutes before baking. Lightly oil and line a 28 x 18 x 2.5 cm/11 x 7 x 1 inch cake tin with nonstick baking parchment. Beat the butter and sugar together until light and fluffy. Sift in the flours and cocoa powder and mix together to form a soft dough.

Press the mixture evenly over the base of the prepared tin. Prick all over with a fork, then bake on the shelf above the centre of the preheated oven for 15 minutes.

Put the butter, sugar, golden syrup, milk and vanilla extract in a small saucepan and heat gently until melted. Remove from the heat and leave to cool for a few minutes, then stir in the eggs and pour over the base. Sprinkle with the nuts.

Bake in the preheated oven for 25 minutes, or until dark golden brown but still slightly soft. Leave to cool in the tin. When cool, carefully remove from the tin, then cut into 12 squares and serve.

Moist Mocha & Coconut Cake

MAKES 9 SQUARES

3 tbsp ground coffee
5 tbsp hot milk
75 g/3 oz butter
175 g/6 oz golden syrup
25 g/1 oz soft light
   brown sugar

40 g/1½ oz desiccated
   coconut
150 g/5 oz plain flour
25 g/1 oz cocoa powder
½ tsp bicarbonate of soda
2 medium eggs, lightly beaten

2 chocolate flakes,
   to decorate

For the coffee icing:
225 g/8 oz icing sugar, sifted
125 g/4 oz butter, softened

Preheat the oven to 170°C/325°F/Gas Mark 3, 10 minutes before baking. Lightly oil and line a deep 20.5 cm/8 inch square cake tin with nonstick baking parchment. Place the ground coffee in a small bowl and pour over the hot milk. Leave to infuse for 5 minutes, then strain through a tea-strainer or a sieve lined with muslin. You will end up with about 4 tablespoons of liquid. Reserve.

Put the butter, golden syrup, sugar and coconut in a small heavy-based saucepan and heat gently until the butter has melted and the sugar dissolved. Sift the flour, cocoa powder and bicarbonate of soda together and stir into the melted mixture with the eggs and 3 tablespoons of the coffee-infused milk.

Pour the mixture into the prepared tin. Bake on the centre shelf of the preheated oven for 45 minutes, or until the cake is well risen and firm to the touch. Leave in the tin for 10 minutes to cool slightly, then turn out onto a wire rack to cool completely.

For the icing, gradually add the icing sugar to the softened butter and beat together until mixed. Add the remaining 1 tablespoon of coffee-infused milk and beat until light and fluffy.

Carefully spread the coffee icing over the top of the cake, then cut into 9 squares. Decorate each square with a small piece of chocolate flake and serve.

All-in-one Chocolate Fudge Cakes

MAKES 15 SQUARES

175 g/6 oz soft dark
  brown sugar
175 g/6 oz butter, softened
150 g/5 oz self-raising flour
25 g/1 oz cocoa powder
½ tsp baking powder
pinch salt

3 medium eggs,
  lightly beaten
1 tbsp golden syrup

For the fudge topping:
75 g/3 oz granulated sugar
150 ml/¼ pint evaporated milk

175 g/6 oz plain dark
  chocolate, roughly
  chopped
40 g/1½ oz unsalted
  butter, softened
125 g/4 oz soft fudge sweets,
  finely chopped

Preheat the oven to 180°C/350°F/Gas Mark 4, 10 minutes before baking. Oil and line a 28 x 18 x 2.5 cm/11 x 7 x 1 inch cake tin with nonstick baking parchment.

Place the soft brown sugar and butter in a bowl and sift in the flour, cocoa powder, baking powder and salt. Add the eggs and golden syrup, then beat with an electric whisk for 2 minutes, before adding 2 tablespoons of warm water and beating for a further 1 minute.

Turn the mixture into the prepared tin and level the top with the back of a spoon. Bake on the centre shelf of the preheated oven for 30 minutes, or until firm to the touch. Turn the cake out onto a wire rack and leave to cool before removing the baking parchment.

To make the topping, gently heat the sugar and evaporated milk in a saucepan, stirring frequently, until the sugar has dissolved. Bring the mixture to the boil and simmer for 6 minutes without stirring.

Remove the mixture from the heat. Add the chocolate and butter and stir until melted and blended. Pour into a bowl and chill in the refrigerator for 1–2 hours until thickened. Spread the topping over the cake, then sprinkle with the chopped fudge. Cut the cake into 15 squares before serving.

Chocolate Nut Brownies

125 g/4 oz butter
150 g/5 oz soft light brown
    sugar, firmly packed
50 g/2 oz plain dark
    chocolate, roughly
    chopped or broken

2 tbsp smooth peanut butter
2 medium eggs
50 g/2 oz unsalted roasted
    peanuts, finely chopped
100 g/3½ oz self-raising flour

For the topping:
125 g/4 oz plain dark
    chocolate, roughly
    chopped or broken
50 ml/2 fl oz sour cream

Preheat the oven to 180°C/350°F/Gas Mark 4, 10 minutes before baking. Lightly oil and line a 20.5 cm/8 inch square cake tin with greaseproof or baking paper.

Combine the butter, sugar and chocolate in a small saucepan and heat gently until the sugar and chocolate have melted, stirring constantly. Reserve and cool slightly.

Mix together the peanut butter, eggs and peanuts in a large bowl. Stir in the cooled chocolate mixture. Sift in the flour and fold together with a metal spoon or rubber spatula until combined. Pour into the prepared tin and bake in the preheated oven for about 30 minutes until just firm. Cool for 5 minutes in the tin before turning out onto a wire rack to cool.

To make the topping, melt the chocolate in a heatproof bowl over a saucepan of simmering water, making sure that the base of the bowl does not touch the water. Cool slightly, then stir in the sour cream until smooth and glossy. Spread over the brownies, refrigerate until set, then cut into squares. Serve the brownies cold.

Chocolate & Orange Rock Buns

MAKES 12

200 g/7 oz self-raising flour
25 g/1 oz cocoa powder
½ tsp baking powder
125 g/4 oz butter
40 g/1½ oz granulated sugar
50 g/2 oz candied
    pineapple, chopped

50 g/2 oz ready-to-eat dried
    apricots, chopped
50 g/2 oz glacé cherries,
    quartered
1 medium egg
finely grated zest of
    ½ orange

1 tbsp orange juice
2 tbsp demerara sugar

Preheat the oven to 200°C/400°F/Gas Mark 6, 15 minutes before baking. Lightly oil two baking sheets, or line them with nonstick baking parchment. Sift the flour, cocoa powder and baking powder into a bowl. Cut the butter into small squares. Add to the dry ingredients, then, using your hands, rub in until the mixture resembles fine breadcrumbs.

Add the granulated sugar, pineapple, apricots and cherries to the bowl and stir to mix. Lightly beat the egg together with the grated orange zest and juice. Drizzle the egg mixture over the dry ingredients and stir to combine. The mixture should be fairly stiff but not too dry; add a little more orange juice, if needed.

Using two teaspoons, shape the mixture into 12 rough heaps on the prepared baking sheets. Sprinkle generously with the demerara sugar. Bake in the preheated oven for 15 minutes, switching the baking sheets around after 10 minutes. Leave on the baking sheets for 5 minutes to cool slightly, then transfer to a wire rack to cool. Serve warm or cold.

Butterscotch Loaf

SERVES 8

1 banana, peeled, weighing
about 100 g/3½ oz
125 g/4 oz soft margarine
125 g/4 oz golden
caster sugar
2 medium eggs

1 tsp almond extract
½ tsp vanilla extract
125 g/4 oz self-raising flour
75 g/3 oz dark
chocolate chips
75 g/3 oz walnuts, chopped

To decorate:
50 g/2 oz natural icing sugar
25 g/1 oz golden lump sugar

Preheat the oven to 170°C/325°F/Gas Mark 3. Grease and line the base of a 1 kg/2 lb 3 oz loaf tin with a long thin strip of nonstick baking parchment.

Place the banana in a bowl and mash. Add the margarine, sugar and eggs along with the extracts and sift in the flour. Beat until smooth, then stir in the chocolate chips and add half the chopped walnuts. Stir until smooth, then spoon into the tin and spread level.

Bake for about 45 minutes until a skewer inserted into the centre comes out clean. Leave in the tin for 5 minutes, then turn out to cool on a wire rack, peel away the paper and leave to cool.

To decorate, make the icing sugar into a runny consistency with 2 teaspoons water. Drizzle over the cake and sprinkle over the remaining walnuts and the sugar lumps. Leave to set for 30 minutes, then serve sliced.

Marmalade Loaf Cake

SERVES 8–10

175 g/6 oz natural golden
caster sugar
175 g/6 oz butter, softened
3 medium eggs, beaten
175 g/6 oz self-raising flour

finely grated zest and juice
of 1 orange
100 g/3½ oz orange
marmalade

For the topping:
zest and juice of 1 orange
125 g/4 oz icing sugar

Preheat the oven to 180°C/350°F/Gas Mark 4. Grease and line a 1 kg/2 lb 3 oz loaf tin with a long thin strip of nonstick baking parchment.

Place the sugar and butter in a bowl and whisk until light and fluffy. Add the beaten egg a little at a time, adding 1 teaspoon flour with each addition.

Add the remaining flour to the bowl with the orange zest, 2 tablespoons orange juice and the marmalade. Using a large metal spoon, fold the mixture together using a figure-of-eight movement until all the flour is incorporated. Spoon the batter into the tin and smooth level.

Bake for about 40 minutes until firm in the centre and a skewer inserted into the centre comes out clean. Cool in the tin for 5 minutes, then turn out to cool on a wire rack.

To make the topping, peel thin strips of zest away from the orange and set aside. Squeeze the juice from the orange. Sift the icing sugar into a bowl and mix with 1 tablespoon orange juice until a thin smooth consistency forms. Drizzle over the top of the cake, letting it run down the sides. Scatter over the orange zest and leave to set for 1 hour.

Fruit & Spice Chocolate Slice

MAKES 10 SLICES

350 g/12 oz self-raising flour
1 tsp ground mixed spice
175 g/6 oz butter, chilled
125 g/4 oz dark chocolate,
    roughly chopped

125 g/4 oz dried mixed fruit
75 g/3 oz dried
    apricots, chopped
75 g/3 oz mixed
    nuts, chopped

175 g/6 oz demerara sugar
2 medium eggs,
    lightly beaten
150 ml/¼ pint milk

Preheat the oven to 180°C/350°F/Gas Mark 4, 10 minutes before baking. Oil and line a deep 18 cm/7 inch square cake tin with nonstick baking parchment. Sift the flour and mixed spice into a large bowl. Cut the butter into small squares and, using your hands, rub in until the mixture resembles fine breadcrumbs.

Add the chocolate, dried mixed fruit, apricots and nuts to the dry ingredients. Reserve 1 tablespoon of the sugar, then add the rest to the bowl and stir together. Add the eggs and half of the milk and mix together, then add enough of the remaining milk to give a soft dropping consistency.

Spoon the mixture into the prepared tin, level the surface with the back of a spoon and sprinkle with the reserved demerara sugar. Bake on the centre shelf of the preheated oven for 50 minutes. Cover the top with kitchen foil to prevent the cake from browning too much and bake for a further 30–40 minutes until it is firm to the touch and a skewer inserted into the centre of the cake comes out clean.

Leave the cake in the tin for 10 minutes to cool slightly, then turn out onto a wire rack and leave to cool completely. Cut into 10 slices and serve.

Cupcakes & Muffins

Madeleine Cupcakes

125 g/4 oz self-raising flour
125 g/4 oz butter, softened
125 g/4 oz golden caster sugar
2 medium eggs, beaten
1 tsp vanilla extract

To decorate:
4 tbsp seedless raspberry jam
65 g/2½ oz desiccated
   coconut
glacé cherries, halved

Preheat the oven to 180°C/350°F/Gas Mark 4. Line a 12-hole muffin tray with 10–12 paper cases, depending on the depth of the holes.

Sift the flour into a bowl and add the butter, sugar, eggs and extract. Beat for about 2 minutes until smooth, then spoon into the paper cases.

Bake in the centre of the oven for about 14–16 minutes until well risen and springy in the centre. Transfer to a wire rack to cool.

To decorate the cupcakes, warm the raspberry jam in a small pan or in the microwave oven in a heatproof dish on low for a few seconds. Brush the warmed jam over the top of each cupcake. Lightly coat the top of each cupcake with coconut, then finish with a halved cherry.

Double Cherry Cupcakes

**MAKES 12 LARGE
CUPCAKES OR
18 FAIRY CAKES**

50 g/2 oz glacé
  cherries, washed,
  dried and chopped
125 g/4 oz self-raising flour
25 g/1 oz dried
  morello cherries

125 g/4 oz soft margarine
125 g/4 oz caster sugar
2 medium eggs
½ tsp almond extract

To decorate:
125 g/4 oz fondant
  icing sugar
pale pink liquid food
  colouring
40 g/1½ oz glacé cherries

Preheat the oven to 190°C/375°F/Gas Mark 5. Line a 12-hole muffin tray with deep paper cases, or two trays with 18 fairy-cake cases.

Dust the chopped glacé cherries lightly in a tablespoon of the flour, then mix with the morello cherries and set aside. Sift the rest of the flour into a bowl, then add the margarine, sugar, eggs and almond extract. Beat for about 2 minutes until smooth, then fold in the cherries.

Spoon the batter into the paper cases and bake for 15–20 minutes until well risen and springy in the centre. Turn out to cool on a wire rack.

To decorate the cupcakes, trim the tops level. Mix the icing sugar with 2–3 teaspoons warm water and a few drops of pink food colouring to make a thick consistency. Spoon the icing over each cupcake filling right up to the edge. Chop the cherries finely and sprinkle over the icing. Leave to set for 30 minutes.

Raspberry Butterfly Cupcakes

MAKES 12–14

125 g/4 oz caster sugar
125 g/4 oz soft tub margarine
2 medium eggs
125 g/4 oz self-raising flour
½ tsp baking powder
½ tsp vanilla extract

To decorate:
4 tbsp seedless raspberry jam
12–14 fresh raspberries
icing sugar, to dust

Preheat the oven to 190˚C/375˚F/Gas Mark 5. Line one or two bun trays with 12–14 paper cases, depending on the depth of the holes.

Place all the cupcake ingredients in a large bowl and beat with an electric mixer for about 2 minutes until smooth. Fill the paper cases halfway up with the mixture.

Bake for about 15 minutes until firm, risen and golden. Remove to a wire rack to cool. When cold, cut a small circle out of the top of each cupcake and then cut the circle in half to form wings.

Fill each cupcake with a teaspoon of raspberry jam. Replace the wings at an angle and top each with a fresh raspberry. Dust lightly with icing sugar and serve immediately.

Fondant Fancies

150 g/5 oz self-raising flour
150 g/5 oz caster sugar
50 g/2 oz ground almonds
150 g/5 oz butter, softened
3 medium eggs, beaten
4 tbsp milk

To decorate:
450 g/1 lb fondant icing sugar
paste food colourings
selection fancy cake
   decorations

Preheat the oven to 180°C/350°F/Gas Mark 4. Line two 12-hole bun trays with 16–18 paper cases, depending on the depth of the holes.

Sift the flour into a bowl and stir in the caster sugar and almonds. Add the butter, eggs and milk and beat until smooth.

Spoon into the paper cases and bake for 15–20 minutes until golden and firm to the touch. Turn out to cool on a wire rack. When cool, trim the tops flat if they have peaked slightly.

To decorate the cupcakes, make the fondant icing to a thick coating consistency, following the packet instructions. Divide into batches and colour each separately with a little paste food colouring. Keep each bowl covered with a damp cloth until needed. Spoon some icing over each cupcake, being sure to flood it right to the edge. Top each with a fancy decoration and leave to set for 30 minutes.

Almond & Cherry Cupcakes

MAKES 12

50 g/2 oz glacé cherries, plus
  extra for decoration
125 g/4 oz self-raising flour,
  plus extra for dusting

125 g/4 oz soft margarine
125 g/4 oz caster sugar
2 medium eggs
½ tsp almond extract

To decorate:
125 g/4 oz icing sugar
1 tsp lemon juice
pink food colouring

Preheat the oven to 190°C/375°F/Gas Mark 5. Line a 12-hole bun tray with small paper cases. Wash the glacé cherries, then dry them thoroughly. Chop the cherries, then dust lightly in flour and set aside.

Sift the flour into a bowl, then add the margarine, sugar, eggs and extract. Beat until smooth for about 2 minutes, then fold in the chopped cherries.

Spoon into the paper cases. Bake for 15–20 minutes until golden and springy in the centre. Turn out to cool on a wire rack.

To decorate, mix the icing sugar with the lemon juice and 2 teaspoons water to form a smooth glacé icing. Add a little pink food colouring and drizzle over the top of each cupcake. Place a halved cherry on top and leave to set for 30 minutes.

Shaggy Coconut Cupcakes

MAKES 12

½ tsp baking powder
200 g/7 oz self-raising flour
175 g/6 oz caster sugar
2 tbsp desiccated coconut
175 g/6 oz soft margarine
3 medium eggs, beaten
2 tbsp milk

To decorate:
1 batch buttercream
  (*see* page 32)
1 tbsp coconut
  liqueur (optional)
175 g/6 oz large shredded
  coconut strands

Preheat the oven to 180°C/350°F/Gas Mark 4. Line a 12-hole deep muffin tray with paper cases.

Sift the baking powder and flour into a large bowl. Add all the remaining ingredients and beat for about 2 minutes until smooth and creamy. Divide evenly between the paper cases.

Bake for 18–20 minutes until risen, golden and firm to the touch. Leave in the muffin trays for 2 minutes, then turn out to cool on a wire rack.

To decorate the cupcakes, if you are using the coconut liqueur, beat this into the buttercream and then swirl over each cupcake. To decorate, press large strands of shredded coconut into the buttercream.

Coffee & Walnut Fudge Cupcakes

MAKES 16–18

125 g/4 oz self-raising flour
125 g/4 oz butter, softened
125 g/4 oz golden
    caster sugar
2 medium eggs
1 tbsp golden syrup

50 g/2 oz walnuts,
    finely chopped

To decorate:
225 g/8 oz golden icing sugar
125 g/4 oz unsalted butter, at

room temperature
2 tsp coffee extract
16–18 small walnut pieces

Preheat the oven to 200°C/400°F/Gas Mark 6. Line two 12-hole bun trays with 16–18 small foil cases, depending on the depth of the tray holes.

Sift the flour into a bowl and add the butter, sugar, eggs and syrup. Beat for about 2 minutes, then fold in the walnuts.

Spoon the mixture into the paper cases and bake for about 12–14 minutes until well risen and springy in the centre. Remove to a wire rack to cool.

Make the frosting by sifting the icing sugar into a bowl. Add the butter, coffee extract and 1 tablespoon hot water. Beat until light and fluffy, then place in a piping bag fitted with a star nozzle. Pipe a swirl on each cupcake and top with a walnut piece.

Chocolate Mud Cupcakes

MAKES 16

150 g/5 oz butter, softened
150 g/5 oz golden
  caster sugar
3 medium eggs, beaten
125 g/4 oz self-raising flour
25 g/1 oz cocoa powder

To decorate:
75 g/3 oz milk chocolate
75 g/3 oz unsalted
  butter, softened
150 g/5 oz golden icing
  sugar, sifted

white and dark chocolate
  sprinkles

Preheat the oven to 190˚C/375˚F/Gas Mark 5. Line one or two bun trays with 16 foil or paper cases.

Place the butter, caster sugar and eggs in a large bowl and then sift in the flour and cocoa powder. Whisk together for about 2 minutes until smooth, then spoon into the cases, filling them two-thirds full.

Bake for about 14 minutes until well risen and springy to the touch. Cool on a wire rack.

To make the frosting, break the chocolate into squares and melt in a heatproof bowl over a pan of barely simmering water. Set aside to cool. Beat the butter and icing sugar together until fluffy, then whisk in the cooled melted chocolate. Swirl over the cupcakes with a flat-bladed knife. Scatter over the sprinkles.

Chocolate Fudge Flake Cupcakes

125 g/4 oz self-raising flour
25 g/1 oz cocoa powder
125 g/4 oz soft margarine
125 g/4 oz soft light
   brown sugar

2 medium eggs, beaten
2 tbsp milk

To decorate:
25 g/1 oz butter

50 g/2 oz golden syrup
15 g/½ oz cocoa powder
125 g/4 oz golden icing sugar
25 g/1 oz cream cheese
40 g/1½ oz chocolate flake bars

Preheat the oven to 180°C/350°F/Gas Mark 4. Line a 12-hole muffin tray with deep paper cases, or one or two bun trays with 18 fairy-cake cases.

Sift the flour and cocoa powder into a large bowl, add the margarine, sugar, eggs and milk and whisk with an electric beater for about 2 minutes until smooth.

Divide the mixture between the paper cases and bake for about 20 minutes for the larger cupcakes and 15 minutes for the fairy cakes until a skewer inserted into the centre comes out clean. Turn out to cool on a wire rack.

To make the topping, melt the butter with the syrup and cocoa powder in a pan. Cool, then whisk in the icing sugar until the mixture has thickened and beat in the cream cheese. Spread the frosting over the cupcakes. Chop the flake bar into small chunks, then place one chunk in the centre of each cupcake.

Chocolate & Cranberry Cupcakes

MAKES 12

175 g/6 oz self-raising flour
25 g/1 oz cocoa powder
1 tsp baking powder
125 g/4 oz soft margarine
125 g/4 oz golden
    caster sugar

2 medium eggs
2 tbsp milk
125 g/4 oz milk
    chocolate chips
50 g/2 oz dried
    cranberries

To decorate:
25 g/1 oz cocoa powder
40 g/1½ oz unsalted butter
125 g/4 oz golden icing sugar
25 g/1 oz dried cranberries

Preheat the oven to 180˚C/350˚F/Gas Mark 4. Line a 12-hole muffin tray with deep paper cases.

Sift the flour, cocoa powder and baking powder into a large bowl, then add the margarine, sugar and eggs. Add the milk and beat until smooth, then fold in the chocolate chips and cranberries.

Spoon into the paper cases and bake for 15–20 minutes until firm in the centre. Remove to a wire rack to cool.

To decorate the cupcakes, blend the cocoa powder with 1 tablespoon hot water until smooth. Cool for 5 minutes. Beat the butter and icing sugar together and then beat in the cocoa mixture. Place in a piping bag with a plain nozzle and pipe swirls on top of each cupcake. Top with dried cranberries.

Chocolate & Toffee Cupcakes

MAKES 12–14

125 g/4 oz soft fudge
125 g/4 oz soft margarine
125 g/4 oz golden
    caster sugar

150 g/5 oz self-raising flour
2 tbsp cocoa powder
2 medium eggs
1 tbsp golden syrup

1 batch cream cheese
    frosting (*see* page 32),
    to decorate

Preheat the oven to 180°C/350°F/Gas Mark 4. Line one or two bun trays with 12–14 paper cases, depending on the depth of the holes. Cut one quarter of the fudge into slices for decoration. Chop the rest into small cubes. Set all the fudge aside.

Place the margarine and the sugar in a large bowl and then sift in the flour and cocoa powder. In another bowl, beat the eggs with the syrup, then add to the flour mixture. Whisk together with an electric beater for 2 minutes, or by hand with a wooden spoon until smooth. Gently fold in the fudge cubes.

Spoon the mixture into the cases, filling them three-quarters full. Bake for about 15 minutes until a skewer inserted into the centre comes out clean. Turn out to cool on a wire rack.

Swirl the cream cheese frosting over each cupcake, then finish by topping with a fudge slice.

Cappuccino Muffins

MAKES 12–14

125 g/4 oz soft margarine
125 g/4 oz golden caster sugar
150 g/5 oz self-raising flour
2 tbsp cocoa powder

2 medium eggs
1 tbsp golden syrup
50 g/2 oz finely
    grated chocolate

To decorate:
150 ml/¼ pint double cream
½ tsp coffee extract
chocolate sprinkles

Preheat the oven to 180°C/350°F/Gas Mark 4. Line one or two bun trays with 12–14 paper cases or silicone moulds, depending on the depth of the holes.

Place the margarine and the sugar in a large bowl, then sift in the flour and cocoa powder. In another bowl, beat the eggs with the syrup, then add to the flour mixture. Whisk together with an electric beater for 2 minutes, or by hand with a wooden spoon until smooth and then fold in the grated chocolate.

Divide the mixture between the cases, filling them three-quarters full. Bake for about 20 minutes until springy to the touch in the centre. Turn out to cool on a wire rack.

For the decoration, whisk the cream until it forms soft peaks, then whisk in the coffee extract. Swirl over the tops of the muffins with a small palette knife. Scatter the tops with chocolate sprinkles to serve.

Triple Chocolate Muffins

MAKES 9

50 g/2 oz dark chocolate
1 tbsp milk
75 g/3 oz butter or
　　block margarine
50 g/2 oz milk chocolate

50 g/2 oz white chocolate
200 g/7 oz self-raising flour
½ tsp bicarbonate of soda
125 g/4 oz soft light
　　brown sugar

1 medium egg
150 ml/¼ pint natural yogurt

Preheat the oven to 180°C/350°F/Gas Mark 4. Line nine holes of a 12-hole muffin tray with deep paper cases.

Chop the dark chocolate into rough chunks and place in a small heavy-based pan with the milk and butter. Heat gently until the mixture melts together, then leave to cool.

Chop the milk and white chocolate coarsely and place in a mixing bowl. Sift in the flour and bicarbonate of soda, then stir in the soft light brown sugar.

In another bowl, beat the egg with the yogurt, then add to the dry ingredients in the bowl with the cooled melted mixture and quickly mix together with a fork. Spoon into the cases and bake for about 25 minutes until risen and firm to the touch. Leave in the tray for 2 minutes to firm up and then turn out onto a wire rack to cool.

Orange Drizzle Cupcakes

MAKES 10

75 g/3 oz dark
   chocolate, chopped
125 g/4 oz butter
125 g/4 oz caster sugar

2 medium eggs, beaten
200 g/7 oz self-raising flour
zest of ½ orange, finely grated
5 tbsp thick natural yogurt

To decorate:
1 batch orange-flavoured
   buttercream (*see* page 32)
2 tbsp marmalade

Preheat the oven to 190˚C/375˚F/Gas Mark 5. Grease 10 deep muffin moulds or line a 12-hole muffin tray with 10 deep paper cases.

Melt the chocolate in a heatproof bowl over a pan of warm water or in the microwave oven on low for 30 seconds and leave to cool.

Put the butter and sugar in a large bowl and whisk until light and fluffy. Gradually beat in the eggs, adding a teaspoon of flour with each addition. Beat in the cooled melted chocolate, then sift in the flour. Add the orange zest and yogurt to the bowl and whisk until smooth.

Spoon the mixture into the paper cases and bake for about 25 minutes until well risen and springy to the touch. Leave for 2 minutes in the moulds or tray, then turn out onto a wire rack.

To decorate, fill a piping bag fitted with a star nozzle with the buttercream and pipe swirls on top of each cupcake. Warm the marmalade and place small drizzles around the sides of the cupcakes with a teaspoon.

Colourful Letters

MAKES 12–14

125 g/4 oz self-raising flour
125 g/4 oz caster sugar
125 g/4 oz soft margarine
2 medium eggs, beaten
1 tsp vanilla extract

To decorate:
225 g/8 oz ready-to-roll
    sugarpaste
paste food colourings

350 g/12 oz icing sugar,
    sifted, plus extra
    for dusting
small coloured sweets

Preheat the oven to 180°C/350°F/Gas Mark 4. Line two 12-hole bun trays with
12–14 paper fairy-cake cases or silicone moulds, depending on the depth of the holes.

Sift the flour into a bowl and stir together with the caster sugar. Add the margarine,
eggs and vanilla extract and beat together for about 2 minutes until smooth.

Spoon into the cases and bake for 15–20 minutes until golden and firm to the touch.
Turn out on a wire rack. When cool, trim the tops flat if they have peaked slightly.

To decorate, colour batches of sugarpaste in bright colours. Dust a clean surface lightly
with icing sugar. Roll each colour out thinly and cut out letters using a set of cutters.

Blend the icing sugar with 1 tablespoon water to make a glacé icing of coating consistency.
Spread over the top of each cupcake and place a bright letter in the centre of each one.
Decorate round the edges with coloured sweets and leave the cupcakes to dry for
30 minutes.

Boys' & Girls' Names

MAKES 16–18

175 g/6 oz self-raising flour
175 g/6 oz caster sugar
175 g/6 oz soft margarine
3 medium eggs, beaten
1 tsp vanilla extract

To decorate:
1 batch buttercream
  (*see* page 32)

paste food colourings
sprinkles and decorations
gel writing icing tubes

Preheat the oven to 180°C/350°F/Gas Mark 4. Line two 12-hole bun trays with
16–18 paper fairy-cake cases or silicone moulds, depending on the depth of the holes.

Sift the flour into a bowl and stir together with the caster sugar. Add the margarine, eggs and
vanilla extract and beat together for about 2 minutes until smooth.

Spoon into the cases and bake for 15–20 minutes until golden and firm to the touch.
Turn out on a wire rack. When cool, trim the tops flat if they have peaked slightly.

Divide the buttercream into batches and colour pink, green and yellow. Spread the icing over
the cakes. Coat the edges of each fairy cake with brightly coloured sprinkles, then add a name
in the centre of each one with the writing icing.

Jellybean Cupcakes

MAKES 12–14

125 g/4 oz self-raising flour
125 g/4 oz caster sugar
125 g/4 oz soft margarine
2 medium eggs, beaten
1 tsp vanilla extract

To decorate:
1 batch buttercream
   (*see* page 32)
colourful jellybeans or
   candied jelly shapes

Preheat the oven to 180°C/350°F/Gas Mark 4. Line two 12-hole bun trays with
12–14 paper fairy-cake cases or silicone moulds, depending on the depth of the holes.

Sift the flour into a bowl and stir together with the caster sugar. Add the margarine,
eggs and vanilla extract and beat together for about 2 minutes until smooth.

Spoon into the cases and bake for 15–20 minutes until golden and firm to the touch.
Turn out to cool on a wire rack.

When completely cold, swirl buttercream icing all over the tops of the cupcakes and decorate
by pressing on coloured jellybeans.

Polka Dot Cupcakes

MAKES 12

150 g/5 oz butter, softened
150 g/5 oz caster sugar
175 g/6 oz self-raising flour
3 medium eggs
1 tsp vanilla extract
2 tbsp milk

To decorate:
1 batch cream cheese
　frosting (*see* page 32)
125 g/4 oz ready-to-roll
　sugarpaste
paste food colourings

Preheat the oven to 180°C/350°F/Gas Mark 4. Line a 12-hole muffin tray with paper or silicone cases.

Cream together the butter and sugar in a bowl, then sift in the flour. In another bowl, beat the eggs with the vanilla extract and milk, then add to the flour mixture and beat until smooth. Spoon into the cases, filling them three-quarters full.

Bake for about 18 minutes until firm to the touch in the centre. Turn out to cool on a wire rack.

To decorate the cupcakes, swirl the top of each cupcake with a little cream cheese icing, using a small palette knife. Divide the sugarpaste into batches and colour each one separately with paste food colouring. Dust a clean flat surface with icing sugar. Roll out the coloured icing and stamp out small coloured circles with the flat end of an icing nozzle. Press the dots onto the frosting.

Pistachio Muffins

MAKES 10

125 g/4 oz self-raising flour
125 g/4 oz butter, softened
125 g/4 oz golden
 caster sugar
2 medium eggs, beaten
1 tbsp maple syrup or
 golden syrup

50 g/2 oz pistachio nuts,
 roughly chopped

To decorate:
225 g/8 oz golden icing sugar
125 g/4 oz unsalted
 butter, softened

2 tsp lemon juice
25 g/1 oz pistachio
 nuts, chopped

Preheat the oven to 200°C/400°F/Gas Mark 6. Line a deep 12-hole muffin tray with 10 deep paper cases.

Sift the flour into a bowl and add the butter, sugar and eggs. Beat for about 2 minutes, then fold in the syrup and chopped nuts.

Spoon the mixture into the paper cases and bake for about 20 minutes until well risen and springy in the centre. Remove to a wire rack to cool.

To decorate the cakes, sift the icing sugar into a bowl, then add the butter, lemon juice and 1 tablespoon hot water. Beat until light and fluffy, then swirl onto each cupcake with a small palette knife. Place the chopped pistachio nuts in a small shallow bowl. Dip the top of each muffin into the nuts to make an attractive topping.

Chocolate Chip Cherry Muffins

MAKES 12

75 g/3 oz glacé cherries
75 g/3 oz milk or dark
   chocolate chips
75 g/3 oz soft margarine

200 g/7 oz caster sugar
2 medium eggs
150 ml/¼ pint thickset
   natural yogurt

5 tbsp milk
275 g/10 oz plain flour
1 tsp bicarbonate of soda

Preheat the oven to 200°C/400°F/Gas Mark 6. Line a deep 12-hole muffin tray with deep paper cases. Wash and dry the cherries. Chop them roughly, mix them with the chocolate chips and set aside.

Beat the margarine and sugar together, then whisk in the eggs, yogurt and milk. Sift in the flour and bicarbonate of soda. Stir until just combined.

Fold in three quarters of the cherries and chocolate chips. Spoon the mixture into the cases, filling them two-thirds full. Sprinkle the remaining cherries and chocolate chips over the top.

Bake for about 20 minutes until golden and firm. Leave in the tins for 4 minutes, then turn out to cool on a wire rack.

Biscuits
& Cookies

Traffic Lights

MAKES 14

125 g/4 oz butter, softened
75 g/3 oz caster sugar
25 g/1 oz golden syrup
1 medium egg, beaten
few drops vanilla extract
275 g/10 oz plain flour, plus
   extra for dusting
1 tsp baking powder

To decorate:
4 tbsp strawberry jam
4 tbsp apricot jam
4 tbsp lime marmalade
icing sugar, for dredging

Preheat the oven to 180°C/350°F/Gas Mark 4. Grease two baking trays. Beat the butter, sugar and syrup together until light and fluffy.

Gradually beat in the egg and vanilla extract. Sift the flour and baking powder into the bowl and stir into the mixture. Gather the mixture up with your hands and work it into a dough. Turn out onto a floured surface and knead gently until smooth. Wrap in clingfilm for 30 minutes and chill.

Roll the pastry out to a thickness of 3 mm/⅛ inch and cut into 28 oblongs measuring 3 x 8.5 cm/1¼ x 3½ inches. Using the broad end of a piping nozzle or a cutter measuring 2 cm/¾ inch wide, cut out three holes in each of 14 of the oblongs, remove the cut-out discs and discard or re-roll to use as pastry trimmings. Place all the oblongs on the baking sheets and bake for 8–10 minutes until golden. Transfer to a wire rack to cool.

Place 3 small teaspoonfuls of different coloured jams along the centre of each rectangular biscuit, starting with strawberry for red at the top, apricot for amber in the middle and lime marmalade for green at the base. Dust the biscuits with the round holes with icing sugar. Position these over the jam on the rectangular biscuits and press down so that the jam shows through.

Cherry Garlands

MAKES 30

125 g/4 oz plain flour
pinch salt
65 g/2½ oz butter, softened
50 g/2 oz caster sugar
1 egg yolk
½ tsp almond extract

To decorate:
12 glacé cherries
1 egg white, lightly beaten
caster sugar

Preheat the oven to 190°C/375°F/Gas Mark 5 and grease two baking sheets. Sift the flour and salt into a bowl or a food processor, add the butter and rub in with fingertips or process until the mixture resembles fine crumbs. Stir in the sugar.

In another bowl, beat the egg yolk with the almond extract and add to the flour mixture. Stir to make a soft dough, then knead lightly. Roll the dough into pea-size balls and arrange 8 balls in a ring on a baking sheet, pressing them together lightly.

Continue making rings until all the dough is used up. Cut each glacé cherry into 8 tiny wedges and place 3 on each biscuit between the balls.

Bake for 14 minutes until golden, remove the biscuits from the oven and brush with beaten egg white. Sprinkle the tops lightly with caster sugar and return to the oven for 2 minutes until a sparkly glaze has formed. Leave to stand on the baking sheets for 2 minutes, then cool completely on a wire rack.

Lemon Butter Biscuits

MAKES 14–18

175 g/6 oz butter, softened
75 g/3 oz caster sugar

175 g/6 oz plain flour
75 g/3 oz cornflour

zest of 1 lemon, finely grated
2 tbsp caster sugar, to decorate

Preheat the oven to 170°C/325°F/Gas Mark 3. Grease two baking sheets. Place the butter into a bowl and beat together with the sugar until light and fluffy.

Sift in the flour and cornflour, add the lemon zest and mix together with a flat-bladed knife to form a soft dough.

Place the dough on a lightly floured surface, knead lightly and roll out thinly. Use biscuit cutters to cut out fancy shapes, re-rolling the trimmings to make more biscuits. Carefully lift each biscuit onto a baking sheet with a palette knife, then prick lightly with a fork.

Bake for 12–15 minutes. Cool on the baking sheets for 5 minutes, then place on a wire rack. Once completely cool, dust with caster sugar.

Oatmeal Raisin Cookies

MAKES 24

175 g/6 oz plain flour
150 g/5 oz rolled oats
1 tsp ground ginger
½ tsp baking powder

½ tsp bicarbonate of soda
125 g/4 oz soft light
  brown sugar
50 g/2 oz raisins

1 medium egg, lightly beaten
150 ml/¼ pint vegetable or
  sunflower oil
4 tbsp milk

Preheat the oven to 200°C/400°F/Gas Mark 6, 15 minutes before baking. Lightly oil a baking sheet.

Mix together the flour, oats, ground ginger, baking powder, bicarbonate of soda, sugar and raisins in a large bowl.

In another bowl, mix the egg, oil and milk together. Make a well in the centre of the dry ingredients and pour in the egg mixture.

Mix the mixture together well with either a fork or a wooden spoon to make a soft but not sticky dough.

Place spoonfuls of the dough well apart on the oiled baking sheet and flatten the tops down slightly with the tines of a fork.

Transfer the biscuits to the preheated oven and bake for 10–12 minutes until golden.

Remove from the oven, leave to cool for 2–3 minutes, then transfer the biscuits to a wire rack to cool.

Oatmeal Coconut Cookies

MAKES 40

225 g/8 oz butter or
   margarine
125 g/4 oz soft light
   brown sugar

125 g/4 oz caster sugar
1 large egg, lightly beaten
1 tsp vanilla extract
225 g/8 oz plain flour

1 tsp baking powder
½ tsp bicarbonate of soda
125 g/4 oz rolled oats
75 g/3 oz desiccated coconut

Preheat the oven to 180°C/350°F/Gas Mark 4, 10 minutes before baking. Lightly oil
a baking sheet.

Cream together the butter or margarine and sugars until light and fluffy. Gradually stir in the
egg and vanilla extract and beat until well blended.

Sift together the flour, baking powder and bicarbonate of soda in another bowl. Add to the
butter and sugar mixture and beat together until smooth. Fold in the rolled oats and coconut
with a metal spoon or rubber spatula.

Roll heaped teaspoonfuls of the mixture into balls and place on the baking sheet about
5 cm/2 inches apart and flatten each ball slightly with the heel of the hand. Transfer to the
preheated oven and bake for 12–15 minutes until just golden.

Remove from the oven and transfer the biscuits to a wire rack to cool completely and serve.

Melting Moments

MAKES 16

125 g/4 oz butter, softened
75 g/3 oz caster sugar
½ tsp vanilla extract
150 g/5 oz self-raising flour
pinch salt

1 small egg or ½ medium
    egg, beaten
25 g/1 oz porridge oats
4 glacé cherries, quartered

Preheat the oven to 180°C/350°F/Gas Mark 4. Grease two baking sheets.

Beat the butter until light and fluffy, then whisk in the caster sugar and vanilla extract.
Sift the flour and salt into the bowl. Add the egg and mix to a soft dough.

Break the dough into 16 pieces and roll each piece into a ball. Spread the oats out on a small
flat bowl or plate. Roll each ball in the oats to coat them all over without flattening them.

Place a cherry quarter in the centre of each ball, then place on the baking sheets, spaced well
apart. Bake for about 15 minutes until risen and golden. Remove from the baking sheets with
a palette knife and cool on a wire rack.

Chocolate Chip Cookies

MAKES 36 BISCUITS

175 g/6 oz plain flour
pinch salt
1 tsp baking powder
¼ tsp bicarbonate of soda
75 g/3 oz butter or margarine

50 g/2 oz soft light
   brown sugar
3 tbsp golden syrup
125 g/4 oz chocolate chips

Preheat the oven to 190°C/375°F/Gas Mark 5, 10 minutes before baking. Lightly oil a large baking sheet.

In a large bowl, sift together the flour, salt, baking powder and bicarbonate of soda.

Cut the butter or margarine into small pieces and add to the flour mixture. Using two knives or the fingertips, rub in the butter or margarine until the mixture resembles coarse breadcrumbs.

Add the light brown sugar, golden syrup and chocolate chips. Mix together until a smooth dough forms.

Shape the mixture into small balls and arrange on the baking sheet, leaving enough space to allow them to expand. (These cookies do not increase in size by a great deal, but allow a little space for expansion.) Flatten the mixture slightly with the fingertips or the heel of the hand.

Bake in the preheated oven for 12–15 minutes until golden and cooked through. Allow to cool slightly, then transfer the biscuits onto a wire rack to cool.

White Chocolate Cookies

MAKES ABOUT 24

130 g/4½ oz butter
40 g/1½ oz caster sugar
60 g/2½ oz soft dark
   brown sugar

1 medium egg
125 g/4 oz plain flour
½ tsp bicarbonate of soda
few drops vanilla extract

150 g/5 oz white chocolate
50 g/2 oz whole
   hazelnuts, shelled

Preheat the oven to 180°C/350°F/Gas Mark 4, 10 minutes before baking. Lightly butter several baking sheets with 15 g/½ oz of the butter. Place the remaining butter with both sugars into a large bowl and beat with a wooden spoon or an electric mixer until soft and fluffy.

Beat the egg, then gradually beat into the creamed mixture. Sift the flour and bicarbonate of soda together, then carefully fold into the creamed mixture with a few drops of vanilla extract.

Roughly chop the chocolate and hazelnuts into small pieces, add to the bowl and gently stir into the mixture. Mix together lightly to blend.

Spoon heaped teaspoons of the mixture onto the prepared baking sheets, making sure that there is plenty of space in between each one as they will spread a lot during cooking.

Bake the cookies in the preheated oven for 10 minutes or until golden, then remove from the oven and leave to cool for 1 minute. Using a spatula, carefully transfer to a wire rack and leave to cool completely.

Chocolate & Vanilla Rings

MAKES 26

175 g/6 oz butter, softened
125 g/4 oz caster sugar
few drops vanilla extract

250 g/9 oz plain flour
15 g/½ oz cocoa powder
25 g/1 oz ground almonds

Preheat the oven to 180°C/350°F/Gas Mark 4 and grease two baking sheets.

Put the butter and sugar in a bowl and beat until light and fluffy. Add the vanilla extract, sift in the flour and mix to a soft dough. Divide the dough in two and add the cocoa powder to one half and the almonds to the other.

Knead each piece of dough separately into a smooth ball, wrap and chill for 30 minutes. Divide each piece into 26 pieces. Take one dark and one light ball and roll each separately into ropes about 12.5 cm/5 inches long using your fingers.

Twist the ropes together to form a circlet and pinch the ends together. Repeat with the remaining dough and place on a greased baking sheet. Bake for 12–14 minutes until risen and firm. Remove to cool on a wire rack.

Peanut Butter Truffle Cookies

MAKES 18

125 g/4 oz dark chocolate
150 ml/¼ pint double cream
125 g/4 oz butter or
    margarine, softened

125 g/4 oz caster sugar
125 g/4 oz crunchy or smooth
    peanut butter
4 tbsp golden syrup

1 tbsp milk
225 g/8 oz plain flour
½ tsp bicarbonate of soda

Preheat the oven to 180°C/350°F/Gas Mark 4, 10 minutes before baking. Make the chocolate filling by breaking the chocolate into small pieces and placing in a heatproof bowl.

Put the double cream into a saucepan and heat to boiling point. Immediately pour over the chocolate. Leave to stand for 1–2 minutes, then stir until smooth. Set aside to cool until firm enough to scoop. Do not refrigerate.

Lightly oil a baking sheet. Cream together the butter or margarine and the sugar until light and fluffy. Blend in the peanut butter, followed by the golden syrup and milk.

Sift together the flour and bicarbonate of soda. Add to the peanut butter mixture, mix well and knead until smooth.

Flatten 1–2 tablespoons of the cookie mixture on a chopping board. Put a spoonful of the chocolate mixture into the centre of the cookie dough, then fold the dough around the chocolate to enclose completely.

Put the balls onto the baking sheet and flatten slightly. Bake in the preheated oven for 10–12 minutes until golden. Remove from the oven and transfer to a wire rack to cool completely and serve.

Chewy Choc & Nut Cookies

MAKES 18

15 g/½ oz butter
4 medium egg whites
350 g/12 oz icing sugar
75 g/3 oz cocoa powder

2 tbsp plain flour
1 tsp instant coffee powder
125 g/4 oz walnuts,
   finely chopped

Preheat the oven to 180°C/350°F/Gas Mark 4, 10 minutes before baking. Lightly grease several baking sheets with the butter and line with a sheet of nonstick baking parchment. Place the egg whites in a large grease-free bowl and whisk with an electric mixer until the egg whites are very frothy.

Add the sugar with the cocoa powder, flour and coffee powder and whisk again until the ingredients are blended thoroughly. Add 1 tablespoon of water and continue to whisk on the highest speed until the mixture is very thick. Fold in the chopped walnuts.

Place tablespoons of the mixture onto the prepared baking sheets, leaving plenty of space between them, as they expand greatly during cooking.

Bake in the preheated oven for 12–15 minutes until the tops are firm, golden and quite cracked. Leave to cool for 30 seconds, then, using a spatula, transfer to a wire rack and leave to cool.

Fudgy Chocolate Tiffin Bars

MAKES 14

25 g/1 oz glacé cherries
60 g/2½ oz shelled hazelnuts
150 g/5 oz dark chocolate

150 g/5 oz unsalted butter
¼ tsp salt
150 g/5 oz digestive biscuits

1 tbsp icing sugar,
   sifted (optional)

Preheat the oven to 180°C/350°F/Gas Mark 4, 10 minutes before required. Lightly oil a 18 cm/7 inch square cake tin and line the base with nonstick baking parchment. Rinse the glacé cherries thoroughly, dry well on absorbent kitchen paper and reserve.

Place the nuts on a baking tray and roast in the preheated oven for 10 minutes, or until light golden brown. Leave to cool slightly, then chop roughly and reserve.

Break the chocolate into small pieces and place with the butter and salt into the top of a double boiler or in a bowl set over a saucepan of gently simmering water. Heat gently, stirring, until melted and smooth. Alternatively, melt the chocolate in the microwave, according to the manufacturer's instructions.

Chop the biscuits into 5 mm/¼ inch pieces and cut the cherries in half. Add to the chocolate mixture with the nuts and stir well. Spoon the mixture into the prepared tin and level the top.

Chill in the refrigerator for 30 minutes, remove from the tin, discard the baking parchment and cut into 14 bars. Cover lightly, return to the refrigerator and keep chilled until ready to serve. To serve, lightly sprinkle the bars with sifted icing sugar, if using.

Miracle Bars

MAKES 12

100 g/3½ oz butter, melted,
plus 1–2 tsp extra
for oiling
125 g/4 oz digestive
biscuit crumbs

175 g/6 oz chocolate chips
75 g/3 oz shredded or
desiccated coconut
125 g/4 oz chopped
mixed nuts

400 g can sweetened
condensed milk

Preheat the oven to 180°C/350°F/Gas Mark 4, 10 minutes before baking. Generously butter a 23 cm/9 inch square cake tin and line with nonstick baking paper.

Pour the butter into the prepared tin and sprinkle the biscuit crumbs over in an even layer.

Add the chocolate chips, coconut and nuts in even layers and drizzle over the condensed milk.

Transfer the tin to the preheated oven and bake for 30 minutes until golden brown. Allow to cool in the tin, then cut into 12 squares and serve.

Golden Honey Fork Biscuits

**MAKES
20–24 BISCUITS**

125 g/4 oz butter or block
  margarine, diced
125 g/4 oz soft light
  brown sugar

1 medium egg, beaten
½ tsp vanilla extract
2 tbsp clear honey
200 g/7 oz plain flour

½ tsp baking powder
½ tsp ground cinnamon

Preheat the oven to 180°C/350°F/Gas Mark 4. Grease two baking sheets.

Place the butter and sugar in a bowl and beat together until light and fluffy. Beat in the egg, a little at a time, and then beat in the vanilla extract and honey.

Sift the flour, baking powder and cinnamon into the bowl and fold into the mixture with a large metal spoon.

Put heaped teaspoons of the mixture onto the prepared baking sheets, leaving room for them to spread out during baking. Press the top of each round with the tines of a fork to make a light indentation.

Bake for 10–12 minutes until golden. Cool for 2 minutes on the baking sheets, then transfer to a wire rack to cool completely.

Honey & Chocolate Hearts

MAKES ABOUT 20

65 g/2½ oz caster sugar
15 g/½ oz butter
125 g/4 oz thick honey
1 small egg, beaten

pinch salt
1 tbsp mixed peel or
   chopped glacé ginger
¼ tsp ground cinnamon

pinch ground cloves
225 g/8 oz plain flour, sifted
½ tsp baking powder, sifted
75 g/3 oz milk chocolate

Preheat the oven to 220°C/425°F/Gas Mark 7, 15 minutes before baking. Lightly oil two baking sheets. Heat the sugar, butter and honey together in a small saucepan until everything has melted and the mixture is smooth.

Remove from the heat and stir until slightly cooled, then add the beaten egg with the salt and beat well. Stir in the mixed peel or glacé ginger, ground cinnamon, ground cloves, the flour and the baking powder and mix well until a dough is formed. Wrap in clingfilm and chill in the refrigerator for 45 minutes.

Place the chilled dough on a lightly floured surface, roll out to about 5 mm/¼ inch thickness and cut out small heart shapes. Place onto the prepared baking sheets and bake in the preheated oven for 8–10 minutes. Remove from the oven and leave to cool slightly. Using a spatula, transfer to a wire rack until cold.

Melt the chocolate in a heatproof bowl set over a saucepan of simmering water. Alternatively, melt the chocolate in the microwave, according to the manufacturer's instructions, until smooth. Dip one half of each biscuit in the melted chocolate. Leave to set before serving.

Almond Macaroons

rice paper
125 g/4 oz caster sugar
50 g/2 oz ground almonds
1 tsp ground rice

2–3 drops almond extract
1 medium egg white
6 blanched almonds, halved

Preheat the oven to 150°C/300°F/Gas Mark 2, 10 minutes before baking. Line a baking sheet with the rice paper.

Mix the caster sugar, ground almonds, ground rice and almond extract together and reserve.

Whisk the egg white until stiff, then gently fold in the caster sugar mixture with a metal spoon or rubber spatula. Mix to form a stiff but not sticky paste. (If the mixture is very sticky, add a little extra ground almonds.)

Place small spoonfuls of the mixture, about the size of an apricot, well apart on the rice paper. Place half a blanched almond in the centre of each. Place in the preheated oven and bake for 25 minutes, or until just pale golden.

Remove the biscuits from the oven and leave to cool for a few minutes on the baking sheet. Cut or tear the rice paper around the macaroons to release them.

Coconut Macaroons

MAKES 18

rice paper
2 medium egg whites
125 g/4 oz icing sugar
125 g/4 oz desiccated
    coconut

125 g/4 oz ground almonds
zest of ½ lemon or lime,
    finely grated

Preheat the oven to 180°C/350°F/Gas Mark 4. Line two baking sheets with rice paper.

Whisk the egg whites in a clean, dry bowl until soft peaks form. Using a large metal spoon, fold in the icing sugar. Fold in the coconut, almonds and lemon or lime zest until a sticky dough forms.

Heap dessertspoonfuls of the mixture onto the rice paper on the baking sheets. Bake for 10 minutes, then reduce the oven temperature to 150°C/300°F/Gas Mark 2.

Bake for a further 5–8 minutes until firm and golden, then remove to a wire rack to cool, breaking off any excess rice paper.

Whipped Shortbread

MAKES 36

225 g/8 oz butter, softened	hundreds and thousands	silver balls
75 g/3 oz icing sugar	sugar strands	50 g/2 oz icing sugar
175 g/6 oz plain flour	chocolate drops	2–3 tsp lemon juice

Preheat the oven to 180°C/350°F/Gas Mark 4, 10 minutes before baking. Lightly oil a baking sheet.

Cream the butter and icing sugar together until fluffy. Gradually add the flour and continue beating for a further 2–3 minutes until smooth and light.

Roll into balls and place on a baking sheet. Cover half of the dough mixture with hundreds and thousands, sugar strands, chocolate drops or silver balls. Keep the other half plain.

Bake in the preheated oven for 6–8 minutes until the bottoms are lightly browned. Remove from the oven and transfer to a wire rack to cool.

Sift the icing sugar into a small bowl. Add the lemon juice and blend until a smooth icing forms.

Using a small spoon, swirl the icing over the cooled plain cookies. Decorate with the extra hundreds and thousands, sugar strands, chocolate drops or silver balls and serve.

Viennese Fingers

225 g/8 oz butter, softened
75 g/3 oz icing sugar
1 medium egg, beaten

1 tsp vanilla extract
275 g/10 oz plain flour
½ tsp baking powder

To decorate:
4 tbsp sieved apricot jam
225 g/8 oz plain chocolate

Preheat the oven to 180°C/350°F/Gas Mark 4. Grease two baking sheets. Put the butter and icing sugar in a bowl and beat together until soft and fluffy.

Whisk in the egg and vanilla extract with 1 tablespoon of the flour. Sift in the remaining flour and the baking powder and beat with a wooden spoon to make a soft dough.

Place the mixture in a piping bag fitted with a large star nozzle and pipe into 6.5 cm/2½ inch lengths on the baking sheets. Bake for 15–20 minutes until pale golden and firm, then transfer to a wire rack to cool.

When cold, thinly spread one flat side of a biscuit with apricot jam and sandwich together with another biscuit.

To decorate the biscuits, break the chocolate into squares and place in a heatproof bowl and stand this over a pan of simmering water. Stir until the chocolate has melted, then dip the ends of the biscuits into the chocolate to coat. Leave on a wire rack for 1 hour until set.

Shortbread Thumbs

MAKES 12

125 g/4 oz self-raising flour	50 g/2 oz granulated sugar	125 g/4 oz icing sugar
125 g/4 oz butter, softened	25 g/1 oz cornflour, sifted	6 coloured glacé cherries,
25 g/1 oz white vegetable fat	5 tbsp cocoa powder, sifted	rinsed, dried and halved

Preheat the oven to 150°C/300°F/Gas Mark 2, 10 minutes before baking. Lightly oil two baking sheets. Sift the flour into a large bowl, cut 75 g/3 oz of the butter and the white vegetable fat into small cubes, add to the flour, then, using your fingertips, rub in until the mixture resembles fine breadcrumbs.

Stir in the granulated sugar, sifted cornflour and 4 tablespoons of the cocoa powder and bring the mixture together with your hand to form a soft and pliable dough.

Place on a lightly floured surface and shape into 12 small balls. Place onto the baking sheets at least 5 cm/2 inches apart, then press each one with a clean thumb to make a dent.

Bake in the preheated oven for 20–25 minutes until light golden brown. Remove from the oven and leave for 1–2 minutes to cool. Transfer to a wire rack and leave until cold.

Sift the icing sugar and the remaining cocoa powder into a bowl and add the remaining softened butter. Blend to form a smooth and spreadable icing with 1–2 tablespoons of hot water. Spread a little icing over the top of each biscuit and place half a cherry on each. Leave until set before serving.

Pecan Caramel Millionaire's Shortbread

125 g/4 oz butter, softened
2 tbsp smooth peanut butter
75 g/3 oz caster sugar
75 g/3 oz cornflour
175 g/6 oz plain flour

For the topping:
200 g/7 oz caster sugar
125 g/4 oz butter
2 tbsp golden syrup
75 ml/3 fl oz liquid glucose
75 ml/3 fl oz water

400 g can sweetened
    condensed milk
175 g/6 oz pecans,
    roughly chopped
75 g/3 oz dark chocolate
1 tbsp butter

Preheat the oven to 180°C/350°F/Gas Mark 4, 10 minutes before baking. Lightly oil and line an 18 x 28 cm/7 x 11 inch tin with greaseproof or baking paper.

Cream together the butter, peanut butter and sugar until light. Sift in the cornflour and flour together and mix in to make a smooth dough. Press the mixture into the prepared tin and prick all over with a fork. Bake in the preheated oven for 20 minutes until just golden. Remove from the oven.

Meanwhile, for the topping, combine the sugar, butter, golden syrup, glucose, water and milk in a heavy-based saucepan. Stir constantly over a low heat without boiling until the sugar has dissolved. Increase the heat, boil steadily, stirring constantly, for about 10 minutes until the mixture turns a golden caramel colour.

Remove the saucepan from the heat and add the pecans. Pour over the shortbread base immediately. Allow to cool, then refrigerate for at least 1 hour.

Break the chocolate into small pieces and put into a heatproof bowl with the butter. Place over a saucepan of barely simmering water, ensuring that the bowl does not come into contact with the water. Leave until melted, then stir together well. Remove the shortbread from the refrigerator and pour the chocolate evenly over the top, spreading thinly to cover. Leave to set, cut into squares and serve.

Gingerbread Biscuits

**MAKES 20 LARGE OR
28 SMALL BISCUITS**

225 g/8 oz plain flour, plus
   extra for dusting
½ tsp ground ginger
½ tsp mixed spice

½ tsp bicarbonate of soda
75 g/3 oz butter
2 tbsp golden syrup
1 tbsp black treacle

75 g/3 oz soft dark
   brown sugar
50 g/2 oz royal icing sugar,
   to decorate

Preheat the oven to 180°C/350°F/Gas Mark 4 and grease two baking sheets. Sift the flour, spices and bicarbonate of soda into a bowl.

Place the butter, syrup, treacle and sugar in a heavy-based pan with 1 tablespoon water and heat gently until every grain of sugar has dissolved and the butter has melted. Cool for 5 minutes, then pour the melted mixture into the dry ingredients and mix to a soft dough.

Leave the dough, covered, for 30 minutes. Roll out the dough on a lightly floured surface to a 3 mm/⅛ inch thickness and cut out fancy shapes. Gather up the trimmings and re-roll the dough, cutting out more shapes. Place on the baking sheets using a palette knife and bake for about 10 minutes until golden and firm. Be careful not to overcook, as the biscuits will brown quickly.

Decorate the biscuits by mixing the royal icing sugar with enough water to make a piping consistency. Place the icing in a small paper piping bag with the end snipped away and pipe faces and decorations onto the biscuits.

Ginger Snaps

300 g/11 oz butter or
  margarine, softened
225 g/8 oz soft light
  brown sugar
75 g/3 oz black treacle

1 medium egg
400 g/14 oz plain flour
2 tsp bicarbonate of soda
½ tsp salt
1 tsp ground ginger

1 tsp ground cloves
1 tsp ground cinnamon
50 g/2 oz granulated sugar

Preheat the oven to 190°C/375°F/Gas Mark 5, 10 minutes before baking. Lightly oil a baking sheet.

Cream together the butter or margarine and the sugar until light and fluffy.

Warm the treacle in the microwave for 30–40 seconds, then gradually add to the butter mixture with the egg. Beat until well combined.

In a separate bowl, sift the flour, bicarbonate of soda, salt, ground ginger, ground cloves and ground cinnamon. Add to the butter mixture and mix together to form a firm dough.

Chill in the refrigerator for 1 hour. Shape the dough into small balls and roll in the granulated sugar. Place well apart on the oiled baking sheet.

Sprinkle the baking sheet with a little water and transfer to the preheated oven.

Bake for 12 minutes until golden and crisp. Transfer to a wire rack to cool and serve.

Chocolate & Ginger Florentines

MAKES 14-16

40 g/1½ oz butter
5 tbsp double cream
50 g/2 oz caster sugar
65 g/2½ oz chopped almonds

25 g/1 oz flaked almonds
40 g/1½ oz glacé
   ginger, chopped
25 g/1 oz plain flour

pinch salt
150 g/5 oz dark chocolate

Preheat the oven to 180°C/350°F/Gas Mark 4, 10 minutes before baking. Lightly oil several baking sheets. Melt the butter, cream and sugar together in a saucepan and bring slowly to the boil. Remove from the heat and stir in the almonds and the glacé ginger.

Leave to cool slightly, then mix in the flour and the salt. Blend together, then place heaped teaspoons of the mixture on the baking sheets. Make sure they are spaced well apart, as they expand during cooking. Flatten them slightly with the back of a wet spoon.

Bake in the preheated oven for 10–12 minutes until just brown at the edges. Leave to cool slightly. Using a spatula, carefully transfer the Florentines to a wire rack and leave to cool.

Melt the chocolate in a heatproof bowl set over a saucepan of gently simmering water. Alternatively, melt the chocolate in the microwave, according to the manufacturer's instructions, until just liquid and smooth. Spread thickly over one side of the Florentines, then mark wavy lines through the chocolate using a fork and leave until firm.

Classic Flapjacks

MAKES 12

175 g/6 oz butter, plus extra
   for greasing
125 g/4 oz demerara sugar
2 tbsp golden syrup

175 g/6 oz jumbo
   porridge oats
few drops vanilla extract

Preheat the oven to 160°C/325°F/Gas Mark 3. Butter a 20.5 cm/8 inch square baking tin.

Place the butter, sugar and golden syrup in a saucepan and heat gently until the butter has melted and every grain of sugar has dissolved.

Remove from the heat and stir in the oats and vanilla extract. Stir well and then spoon the mixture into the prepared tin.

Smooth level with the back of a large spoon. Bake in the centre of the oven for 30–40 minutes until golden. Leave to cool in the tin for 10 minutes, then mark into fingers and leave in the tin until completely cold. When cold, cut into fingers with a sharp knife.

Fruit & Nut Flapjacks

MAKES 12

75 g/3 oz butter or margarine
125 g/4 oz soft light
   brown sugar
3 tbsp golden syrup

50 g/2 oz raisins
50 g/2 oz walnuts,
   roughly chopped
175 g/6 oz rolled oats

50 g/2 oz icing sugar
1–1½ tbsp lemon juice

Preheat the oven to 180°C/350°F/Gas Mark 4, 10 minutes before baking. Lightly oil a
23 cm/9 inch square cake tin.

Melt the butter or margarine with the sugar and syrup in a small saucepan over a low heat.
Remove from the heat.

Stir the raisins, walnuts and oats into the syrup mixture and mix together well. Spoon evenly
into the prepared tin and press down well. Transfer to the preheated oven and bake for 20–25
minutes.

Remove from the oven and leave to cool in the tin. Cut into bars while still warm.

Sift the icing sugar into a small bowl, then gradually beat in the lemon juice a little at a time
to form a thin icing. Place into an icing bag fitted with a writing nozzle, then pipe thin lines
over the flapjacks. Allow to cool and serve.

Chocolate Orange Biscuits

MAKES 30

100 g/3½ oz dark chocolate
125 g/4 oz butter
125 g/4 oz caster sugar
pinch salt

1 medium egg, beaten
grated zest of 2 oranges
200 g/7 oz plain flour
1 tsp baking powder

125 g/4 oz icing sugar
1–2 tbsp orange juice

Preheat the oven to 200°C/400°F/Gas Mark 6, 15 minutes before baking. Lightly oil several baking sheets. Coarsely grate the chocolate and reserve. Beat the butter and sugar together until creamy. Add the salt, beaten egg and half the orange zest and beat again.

Sift the flour and baking powder, add to the bowl with the grated chocolate and beat to form a dough. Shape into a ball, wrap in clingfilm and chill in the refrigerator for 2 hours.

Roll the dough out on a lightly floured surface to 5 mm/¼ inch thickness and cut into 5 cm/2 inch rounds. Place the rounds on the prepared baking sheets, allowing room for expansion. Bake in the preheated oven for 10–12 minutes until firm. Remove the biscuits from the oven and leave to cool slightly. Using a spatula, transfer to a wire rack and leave to cool.

Sift the icing sugar into a small bowl and stir in sufficient orange juice to make a smooth, spreadable icing. Pipe or spread the icing over the biscuits, leave until almost set, then sprinkle on the remaining grated orange zest before serving.

Chocolate Macaroons

MAKES 20

65 g/2½ oz dark chocolate
125 g/4 oz ground almonds
125 g/4 oz caster sugar
¼ tsp almond extract

1 tbsp cocoa powder
2 medium egg whites
1 tbsp icing sugar

Preheat the oven to 180°C/350°F/Gas Mark 4, 10 minutes before baking. Lightly oil several baking sheets and line with sheets of nonstick baking parchment. Melt the chocolate in a heatproof bowl set over a saucepan of simmering water. Alternatively, melt in the microwave, according to the manufacturer's instructions. Stir until smooth, then cool slightly.

Place the ground almonds in a food processor and add the sugar, almond extract, cocoa powder and 1 of the egg whites. Add the melted chocolate and a little of the other egg white and blend to make a soft, smooth paste. Alternatively, place the ground almonds with the sugar, almond extract and cocoa powder in a bowl and make a well in the centre. Add the melted chocolate with sufficient egg white and gradually blend together to form a smooth but not sticky paste.

Shape the dough into small balls the size of large walnuts and place them on the prepared baking sheets. Flatten them slightly, then brush with a little water. Sprinkle over a little icing sugar and bake in the preheated oven for 10–12 minutes until just firm.

Using a spatula, carefully lift the macaroons off the baking parchment and transfer to a wire rack to cool. These are best served immediately, but can be stored in an airtight container.

Sweet Pies & Puddings

Apple Pie

175 g/6 oz plain flour
pinch salt
40 g/1½ oz lard or white
    vegetable fat
40 g/1½ oz butter or block
    margarine
1 tbsp caster sugar

For the filling:
500 g/1¼ lb cooking apples,
    peeled, cored and sliced
125 g/4 oz caster sugar
1 tsp ground cinnamon
½ tsp ground nutmeg
50 g/2 oz sultanas

15 g/½ oz butter
milk, for glazing
caster sugar, for sprinkling

Sift the flour and salt into a bowl or a food processor and add the fats, cut into small pieces. Rub in with your fingertips, or process, until the mixture resembles fine crumbs. Mix in the sugar and add 2–3 tablespoons cold water to form a soft dough, then knead lightly until smooth. Wrap and chill for 30 minutes.

Preheat the oven to 220°C/425°F/Gas Mark 7 and grease a 1.2 litre/2¼ pint deep pie dish. Roll out the pastry on a lightly floured surface. Turn the pie dish upside down onto the pastry and cut round it to form the lid. Roll the trimmings into a 2.5 cm/1 inch strip and press this firmly onto the top edge of the dish.

Mix the sliced apples with the sugar, spices and sultanas. Place in the dish and then dot with butter. Dampen the pastry edge with water, then place the pastry lid over. Press the edges to seal, and flute together with your thumb and forefinger. Make a hole in the centre to allow the steam to escape, then decorate with pastry trimmings.

Brush with milk, then sprinkle with caster sugar. Bake for 10 minutes, then turn the oven temperature down to 190°C/350°F/Gas Mark 5 and bake for a further 25–30 minutes until crisp and golden. Serve hot straight away with cream or custard.

Crunchy Rhubarb Crumble

SERVES 6

125 g/4 oz plain flour
50 g/2 oz softened butter
50 g/2 oz rolled oats

50 g/2 oz demerara sugar
1 tbsp sesame seeds
½ tsp ground cinnamon

450 g/1 lb fresh rhubarb
50 g/2 oz caster sugar
custard or cream, to serve

Preheat the oven to 180°C/350°F/Gas Mark 4. Place the flour in a large bowl and cut the butter into cubes. Add to the flour and rub in with the fingertips until the mixture looks like fine breadcrumbs, or blend for a few seconds in a food processor.

Stir in the rolled oats, demerara sugar, sesame seeds and cinnamon. Mix well and reserve.

Prepare the rhubarb by removing the thick ends of the stalks and cut diagonally into 2.5 cm/ 1 inch chunks. Wash thoroughly and pat dry with a clean tea towel. Place the rhubarb in a 1.1 litre/2 pint pie dish.

Sprinkle the caster sugar over the rhubarb and top with the reserved crumble mixture. Level the top of the crumble so that all the fruit is well covered and press down firmly. If liked, sprinkle the top with a little extra caster sugar.

Place on a baking sheet and bake in the preheated oven for 40–50 minutes until the fruit is soft and the topping is golden brown. Sprinkle the pudding with some more caster sugar and serve hot with custard or cream.

Rhubarb & Raspberry Cobbler

325 g/11½ oz rhubarb, cut
   into chunks
175 g/6 oz raspberries
50 g/2 oz golden caster sugar
zest and juice of 1 orange

For the topping:
225 g/8 oz plain flour
1 tbsp baking powder
50 g/2 oz butter, diced
50 g/2 oz caster sugar

150 ml/¼ pint milk
custard or double cream,
   to serve

Preheat the oven to 220°C/425°F/Gas Mark 7. Butter a 1.7 litre/3 pint ovenproof dish.

Mix the rhubarb chunks with the raspberries and sugar and place in the buttered dish. Finely grate the zest from the orange and set aside. Squeeze out the juice and add to the dish with the rhubarb. Cover the dish with a piece of foil and bake for 20 minutes.

To make the topping, sift the flour and baking powder into a bowl and stir in the grated orange zest. Rub in the butter with your fingertips until the mixture resembles fine crumbs. Stir in the caster sugar and quickly add the milk. Mix with a fork to make a soft dough. (The mixture has to be made quickly as the raising agent – baking powder – starts to activate as soon as liquid is added.)

Take the dish out of the oven and discard the foil. Break off rough tablespoons of the dough and drop them on top of the fruit filling. Bake for about 25 minutes until the topping is firm and golden. Serve immediately with custard or single cream.

Freeform Fruit Pie

SERVES 6

175 g/6 oz plain flour
40 g/1½ oz lard or white
  vegetable fat
40 g/1½ oz butter
1 tbsp caster sugar
1 medium egg, separated

For the filling:
2 tbsp semolina
600 g/1¼ lb gooseberries
75 g/3 oz caster sugar
zest of 1 orange, finely grated
1 egg, separated

2 tbsp caster sugar
vanilla ice cream, to serve

Sift the flour into a bowl or a food processor and add the fats, cut into small pieces. Rub in with your fingertips, or process, until fine crumbs form. Stir in the sugar and the egg yolk and mix with a few drops of cold water to make a soft dough. Knead lightly, then wrap in clingfilm and chill for 30 minutes.

Preheat the oven to 190˚C/375˚F/Gas Mark 5 and grease a large baking sheet. Roll out the pastry to a circle approximately 30 cm/12 inches wide.

Lift the pastry onto a rolling pin and place on the baking sheet.

Beat the egg yolk and brush this lightly over the pastry. Sprinkle the semolina lightly over the egg yolk.

Mix the gooseberries with the sugar and zest and pile into the centre of the pastry circle, leaving a border of 8 cm/3¾ inches all round.

Gather the pastry edges up over the filling. Press the edges together roughly, leaving the centre exposed. Beat the egg whites until foaming, then brush over the pastry. Scatter over the caster sugar and bake for about 30 minutes until golden. Remove to a serving plate and serve with vanilla ice cream.

Classic Apple Strudel

SERVES 8

700 g/1½ lb cooking apples
zest and juice of 1 orange
50 g/2 oz natural caster sugar
75 g/3 oz raisins
125 g/4 oz butter

50 g/2 oz fresh white
  breadcrumbs
40 g/1½ oz flaked almonds
½ tsp ground cinnamon
350 g/12 oz filo pastry sheets

icing sugar, for dusting
whipped cream, crème
  fraîche or natural yogurt,
  to serve

Preheat the oven to 190°C/375°F/Gas Mark 5 and butter a large baking sheet. Peel, core and slice the apples, finely grate the zest from the orange and squeeze out the juice. Place the apples, orange zest and juice and caster sugar in a pan and cook over a gentle heat for 10 minutes until the apples are tender, then pour into a bowl, stir in the raisins and leave to cool.

Melt 25 g/1 oz of the butter in a nonstick frying pan and add the breadcrumbs. Cook for a minute to brown, then add the almonds and cook for a further minute. Remove from the heat, stir in the cinnamon and leave to cool.

Melt the remaining butter and brush 1 large or 2 small filo sheets overlapping. Reserve 1 sheet for decoration and continue buttering and layering the sheets. Brush the top sheet with butter. Sprinkle over half the breadcrumb mixture, leaving a 5 cm/2 inch border. Top with the cooked apples, then the remaining breadcrumb mixture. Fold in the sides, then roll up to encase the filling. Place on the greased baking sheet seam-side down. Arrange the reserved sheet on top in ruffles and brush the roll all over with butter. Bake for 20–30 minutes until crisp and light golden. Place on a serving dish and dust with icing sugar. Serve sliced with whipped cream, crème fraîche or thick natural yogurt.

Mini Pistachio & Chocolate Strudels

MAKES 24

5 large sheets filo pastry
50 g/2 oz butter, melted
1–2 tbsp caster sugar,
   for sprinkling
50 g/2 oz white chocolate,
   melted, to decorate

For the filling:
125 g/4 oz unsalted
   pistachios, finely chopped
3 tbsp caster sugar
50 g/2 oz dark chocolate,
   finely chopped

1–2 tsp rosewater
1 tbsp icing sugar,
   for dusting

Preheat the oven to 170°C/325°F/Gas Mark 3, 10 minutes before baking. Lightly oil two large baking sheets. For the filling, mix the finely chopped pistachio nuts, the sugar and dark chocolate in a bowl. Sprinkle with the rosewater and stir lightly together and reserve.

Cut each filo pastry sheet into four to make 23 x 18 cm/9 x 7 inch rectangles. Place one rectangle on the work surface and brush with a little melted butter. Place another rectangle on top and brush with a little more butter. Sprinkle with a little caster sugar and spread about 1 dessertspoon of the filling along one short end. Fold the short end over the filling, then fold in the long edges and roll up. Place on the baking sheet seam-side down. Continue with the remaining pastry sheets and filling until both are used.

Brush each strudel with the remaining melted butter and sprinkle with a little caster sugar. Bake in the preheated oven for 20 minutes, or until golden brown and the pastry is crisp.

Remove from the oven and leave on the baking sheet for 2 minutes, then transfer to a wire rack. Dust with icing sugar. Place the melted white chocolate in a small piping bag fitted with a plain writing nozzle and pipe squiggles over the strudels. Leave to set before serving.

'Mars' Bar Mousse in Filo Cups

SERVES 6

6 large sheets filo pastry,
  thawed if frozen
40 g/1½ oz unsalted
  butter, melted
1 tbsp caster sugar
3 x 58 g 'Mars' bars,
  coarsely chopped

1½ tbsp milk
300 ml/½ pint double cream
1 large egg white
1 tsp cocoa powder
1 tbsp dark chocolate, grated
chocolate sauce, to
  serve (optional)

For the topping:
300 ml/½ pint whipping cream
125 g/4 oz white
  chocolate, grated
1 tsp vanilla extract

Preheat the oven to 180°C/350°F/Gas Mark 4, 10 minutes before baking. Lightly oil six 150 ml/¼ pint ramekins. Cut the filo pastry into 15 cm/6 inch squares, place one square on the work surface, brush with a little of the melted butter and sprinkle with a little caster sugar. Butter a second square and lay it over the first at an angle, sprinkle with a little more caster sugar and repeat with two more pastry squares. Press the assembled filo pastry into the oiled ramekin, pressing into the base to make a flat bottom and keeping the edges pointing up. Continue making the cups in this way, then place on a baking sheet and bake in the preheated oven for 10–15 minutes until crisp and golden. Remove and leave to cool before removing the filo cups from the ramekins. Leave until cold.

Melt the 'Mars' bars and milk in a small saucepan, stirring constantly, until melted and smooth. Leave to cool for 10 minutes, stirring occasionally. Whisk the cream until thick and stir a spoonful into the melted 'Mars' bar mixture, then fold in the remaining cream. Whisk the egg white until stiff and fold into the 'Mars' bar mixture together with the cocoa powder. Chill the mousse in the refrigerator for 2–3 hours. For the topping, boil 125 ml/4 fl oz of the whipping cream, add the white chocolate and vanilla extract and stir until smooth, then strain into a bowl and leave to cool. Whisk the remaining cream until thick, then fold into the white chocolate mixture. Spoon the mousse into the filo cups, cover with the cream mixture and sprinkle with grated chocolate. Chill in the refrigerator before serving with chocolate sauce, if liked.

Lemon Meringue Pie

SERVES 4–6

175 g/6 oz plain flour
pinch salt
40 g/1½ oz lard or white
vegetable fat
40 g/1½ oz butter or
block margarine

For the filling:
grated zest and juice
of 2 lemons
75 g/3 oz granulated
sugar
300 ml/½ pint water

40 g/1½ oz cornflour
2 large egg yolks

For the topping:
2 large egg whites
125 g/4 oz caster sugar

Preheat the oven to 200°C/400°F/Gas Mark 6 and place a baking sheet in the oven to heat. Sift the flour and salt into a bowl or a food processor and add the fats, cut into small pieces. Rub in with your fingertips, or process, until the mixture resembles fine crumbs. Mix in 2–3 tablespoons cold water to form a soft dough, then knead lightly until smooth. Grease a 20.5 cm/8 inch round flan tin. Roll out the pastry on a lightly floured surface and use to line the dish. Chill for 30 minutes while you make the filling.

Put the zest and granulated sugar in a pan with 300 ml/½ pint water in a heavy-based pan over a low heat and stir until the sugar has completely dissolved. Blend the cornflour with the lemon juice to a smooth paste, then add to the pan and bring to the boil, stirring all the time. Boil for 2 minutes, then remove from the heat and beat in the egg yolks. Set aside to cool.

Prick the pastry case, line with greaseproof paper and pour in baking beans. Place on the baking sheet and bake for 10 minutes. Remove from the oven and lift out the paper and beans. Bake the pastry for a further 10 minutes. Remove from the oven, spoon the lemon filling into the pastry case and set aside. Reduce the oven temperature to 150°C/300°F/Gas Mark 2.

Whisk the egg whites in a clean, dry bowl until very stiff. Whisk in half the caster sugar a little at a time, then fold in the remainder. Spread over the lemon filling, making sure it covers the top, right to the edges of the filling. Bake for 30 minutes until the meringue is golden. Leave to 'settle' for 20 minutes before serving, or eat cold on the day of baking.

Banoffee Pie

175 g/6 oz plain flour
pinch salt
1 tbsp caster sugar
75 g/3 oz butter, diced
1 egg yolk

For the filling and topping:
75 g/3 oz butter
50 g/2 oz soft light
   brown sugar
225 g/8 oz canned
   condensed milk

2 tbsp milk
3 bananas, peeled and sliced
150 ml/¼ pint double cream
25 g/1 oz plain chocolate,
   grated, to decorate

Sift the flour and salt into a bowl or a food processor and add the sugar and butter. Rub in, or process, until the mixture resembles fine crumbs. Add the egg yolk and a few drops of cold water and mix to a dough. Knead until smooth, then wrap in clingfilm and chill for 30 minutes.

Preheat the oven to 200˚C/400˚F/Gas Mark 6 and grease a 20.5 cm/8 inch round flan tin. Roll the pastry out on a lightly floured surface and use to line the tin. Press the pastry into the sides of the tin and prick the base with a fork. Line the pastry case with greaseproof paper and baking beans, bake for 10 minutes, remove the beans, then bake for a further 5–10 minutes until golden. Place the tin on a wire rack to cool.

Meanwhile, make the filling. Gently heat the butter and sugar in a small pan until the butter melts and all the grains of sugar dissolve. Bring to the boil, then let boil for 1 minute. Remove from the heat and add the condensed milk and the 2 tablespoons milk. Stir together, then bring back to the boil and let boil for 2 minutes, stirring constantly. Remove from the heat. Place the sliced bananas in the pastry case and pour the warm toffee over. Leave to cool for 1 hour. Whip the cream and spread over the cold banoffee filling. Sprinkle with the grated chocolate and serve immediately.

Ricotta Cheesecake
with Strawberry Coulis

125 g/4 oz digestive biscuits
100 g/3½ oz candied
  peel, chopped
65 g/2½ oz butter, melted
150 ml/¼ pint crème fraîche

575 g/1¼ lb ricotta cheese
100 g/3½ oz caster sugar
seeds of 1 vanilla pod
2 large eggs
225 g/8 oz strawberries

25–50 g/1–2 oz caster sugar,
  to taste
zest and juice of 1 orange

Preheat the oven to 170°C/325°F/Gas Mark 3. Line a 20.5 cm/8 inch springform tin with baking parchment. Place the biscuits into a food processor together with the peel. Blend until the biscuits are crushed and the peel is chopped. Add 50 g/2 oz of the melted butter and process until mixed. Tip into the tin and spread evenly over the bottom. Press firmly into place and reserve.

Blend together the crème fraîche, ricotta cheese, sugar, vanilla seeds and eggs in a food processor. With the motor running, add the remaining melted butter and blend for a few seconds. Pour the mixture onto the base. Transfer to the preheated oven and cook for about 1 hour, until set and risen round the edges, but slightly wobbly in the centre. Switch off the oven and allow to cool there. Chill in the refrigerator for at least 8 hours, or preferably overnight.

Wash and drain the strawberries. Hull the fruit and remove any soft spots. Put into the food processor, along with 25 g/1 oz of the sugar and the orange juice and zest. Blend until smooth. Add the remaining sugar to taste. Pass through a sieve to remove seeds and chill in the refrigerator until needed.

Cut the cheesecake into wedges, spoon over some of the strawberry coulis and serve.

Baked Lemon & Sultana Cheesecake

**CUTS INTO
10 SLICES**

275 g/10 oz caster sugar
50 g/2 oz butter
50 g/2 oz self-raising flour
½ level tsp baking powder
5 large eggs
450 g/1 lb cream cheese

40 g/1½ oz plain flour
grated zest of 1 lemon
3 tbsp fresh lemon juice
150 ml/¼ pint crème fraîche
75 g/3 oz sultanas

To decorate:
1 tbsp icing sugar
fresh blackcurrants or
blueberries
mint leaves

Preheat the oven to 170°C/325°F/Gas Mark 3. Oil a 20.5 cm/8 inch loose-bottomed round cake tin with nonstick baking paper.

Beat 50 g/2 oz of the sugar and the butter together until light and creamy, then stir in the self-raising flour, baking powder and 1 egg. Mix lightly together until well blended. Spoon into the prepared tin and spread the mixture over the base. Separate the 4 remaining eggs and reserve.

Blend the cheese in a food processor until soft. Gradually add the egg yolks and the sugar and blend until smooth. Turn into a bowl and stir in the remaining plain flour, lemon zest and juice. Mix lightly before adding the crème fraîche and sultanas, stirring well.

Whisk the egg whites until stiff, fold into the cheese mixture and pour into the tin. Tap lightly on the work surface to remove any air bubbles. Bake in the preheated oven for about 1 hour, or until golden and firm. Cover lightly if browning too much. Switch the oven off and leave in the oven to cool for 2–3 hours.

Remove the cheesecake from the oven and, when completely cold, remove from the tin. Sprinkle with the icing sugar, decorate with the blackcurrants or blueberries and mint leaves and serve.

Triple Chocolate Cheesecake

SERVES 6

For the base:
150 g/5 oz digestive
   biscuits, crushed
50 g/2 oz butter, melted

For the cheesecake:
75 g/3 oz white chocolate,
   roughly chopped

300 ml/½ pint double cream
50 g/2 oz caster sugar
3 medium eggs, beaten
400 g/14 oz full-fat soft
   cream cheese
2 tbsp cornflour
75 g/3 oz dark chocolate,
   roughly chopped

75 g/3 oz milk chocolate,
   roughly chopped
fromage frais, to serve

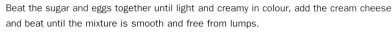

Preheat the oven to 180°C/350°F/Gas Mark 4, 10 minutes before baking. Lightly oil a 23 x 7.5 cm/9 x 3 inch springform tin.

To make the base, mix together the crushed biscuits and melted butter. Press into the base of the tin and leave to set. Chill in the refrigerator.

Place the white chocolate and cream in a small heavy-based saucepan and heat gently until the chocolate has melted. Stir until smooth and reserve.

Beat the sugar and eggs together until light and creamy in colour, add the cream cheese and beat until the mixture is smooth and free from lumps.

Stir the reserved white chocolate cream together with the cornflour into the soft cream cheese mixture. Add the dark and milk chocolate and mix lightly together until blended. Spoon over the chilled base, place on a baking sheet and bake in the preheated oven for 1 hour.

Switch off the heat, open the oven door and leave the cheesecake to cool in the oven. Chill in the refrigerator for at least 6 hours before removing the cheesecake from the tin. Cut into slices and transfer to serving plates. Serve with fromage frais.

Fudgy Mocha Pie with Espresso Custard Sauce

**CUTS INTO
10 SLICES**

125 g/4 oz dark chocolate,
chopped
125 g/4 oz butter, diced
1 tbsp instant espresso powder
4 large eggs
1 tbsp golden syrup
125 g/4 oz sugar
1 tsp ground cinnamon

3 tbsp milk
icing sugar, for dusting
few fresh strawberries,
to serve

For the espresso custard sauce:
2–3 tbsp instant espresso
powder, or to taste

225 ml/8 fl oz prepared
custard sauce
225 ml/8 fl oz single cream
2 tbsp coffee-flavoured
liqueur (optional)

Preheat the oven to 180°C/350°F/Gas Mark 4, 10 minutes before baking. Line with kitchen foil or lightly oil a deep 23 cm/9 inch pie plate. Melt the chocolate and butter in a small saucepan over a low heat and stir until smooth, then reserve. Dissolve the instant espresso powder in 1–2 tablespoons of hot water and reserve.

Beat the eggs with the golden syrup, sugar, dissolved espresso powder, cinnamon and milk until blended. Add the melted chocolate mixture and whisk until blended. Pour into the pie plate.

Bake the pie in the preheated oven for about 20–25 minutes until the edge has set but the centre is still very soft. Leave to cool, remove from the plate, then dust lightly with icing sugar.

To make the custard sauce, dissolve the instant espresso powder with 2–3 tablespoons of hot water, then whisk into the prepared custard sauce. Slowly add the single cream, whisking constantly, then stir in the coffee-flavoured liqueur, if using. Serve slices of the pie in a pool of espresso custard with strawberries.

Mini Strawberry Tartlets

MAKES 12 TARTLETS

225 g/8 oz plain flour
25 g/1 oz icing sugar
125 g/4 oz butter, diced
25 g/1 oz ground almonds
1 egg yolk

For the filling:
85 ml/3 fl oz double cream
175 g/6 oz full-fat cream cheese

25 g/1 oz vanilla caster sugar
2 tbsp amaretto almond-
   flavoured liqueur
250 g/9 oz strawberries,
   hulled, and halved if large
2 tbsp sieved raspberry jam
small mint leaves,
   to decorate

Sift the flour and icing sugar into a bowl and add the diced butter. Rub the butter into the flour with your fingertips until the mixture resembles fine crumbs. Alternatively, place the flour, icing sugar and butter in a food processor and process until fine crumbs form. Stir in the ground almonds and egg yolk and mix with 1 tablespoon cold water to form a soft dough. Cover with clingfilm and chill for 30 minutes.

Preheat the oven to 200°C/400°F/Gas Mark 6 and grease a 12-hole muffin tin. Roll out the dough on a lightly floured surface to 6 mm/¼ inch thickness and cut out twelve 10 cm/4 inch circles. Press the circles into the holes in the tin, loosely fluting up the edges. Prick the bases with a fork and bake for 12–15 minutes until light golden. Leave to cool in the tins for 3 minutes, then remove to cool completely on a wire rack.

To make the filling, whip the cream until stiff then mix with the cream cheese, sugar and liqueur. Chill until needed and then spoon into the pastry cases.

Arrange the fresh strawberries on top and brush lightly with a little jam to glaze. Decorate with small fresh mint leaves and serve immediately.

Goats' Cheese & Lemon Tart

SERVES 8-10

For the pastry:
125 g/4 oz butter, cut into
    small pieces
225 g/8 oz plain flour
pinch salt
50 g/2 oz caster sugar
1 medium egg yolk

For the filling:
350 g/12 oz mild fresh goats'
    cheese, such as Chavroux
3 medium eggs, beaten
150 g/5 oz caster sugar
grated zest and juice
    of 3 lemons

450 ml/¾ pint double cream
fresh raspberries, to decorate
    and serve

Preheat the oven to 200°C/400°F/Gas Mark 6, 15 minutes before cooking. Rub the butter into the plain flour and salt until the mixture resembles breadcrumbs, then stir in the sugar. Beat the egg yolk with 2 tablespoons of cold water and add to the mixture. Mix together until a dough is formed, then turn the dough out onto a lightly floured surface and knead until smooth. Chill in the refrigerator for 30 minutes.

Roll the dough out thinly on a lightly floured surface and use to line a 4 cm/1½ inch deep 23 cm/9 inch fluted flan tin. Chill in the refrigerator for 10 minutes. Line the pastry case with greaseproof paper and baking beans or foil and bake blind in the preheated oven for 10 minutes. Remove the paper and beans or foil. Return to the oven for a further 12–15 minutes until cooked, then remove from the oven and leave to cool slightly. Reduce the oven temperature to 150°C/300°F/Gas Mark 2.

Beat the goats' cheese until smooth. Whisk in the eggs, sugar, lemon zest and juice. Add the cream and mix well.

Carefully pour the cheese mixture into the pastry case and return to the oven. Bake in the oven for 35–40 minutes until just set. If it begins to brown or swell, open the oven door for 2 minutes, then reduce the temperature to 120°C/250°F/Gas Mark ½ and leave the tart to cool in the oven. Chill in the refrigerator until cold. Decorate and serve with fresh raspberries.

Autumn Tart

175 g/6 oz plain flour
pinch salt
1 tbsp caster sugar
75 g/3 oz butter, diced
1 egg yolk

For the filling:
50 g/2 oz butter

50 g/2 oz caster sugar
50 g/2 oz ground almonds
1 egg yolk
2 dessert apples, peeled,
  cored and sliced
4 plums, pitted and sliced
2 tbsp lemon juice
2 tbsp caster sugar

milk, for brushing
crème fraîche, to serve

Sift the flour and salt into a bowl or a food processor, add the sugar and butter and rub in or process until the mixture resembles fine crumbs. Add the egg yolk and 1 tablespoon cold water and mix to a dough. Knead until smooth, then wrap in clingfilm and chill for 30 minutes.

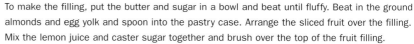

Preheat the oven to 180˚C/350˚F/Gas Mark 4 and grease a 20.5 cm/8 inch round flan tin. Roll the pastry out on a lightly floured surface and use to line the tin. Trim the top and reserve the trimmings. Press the pastry into the sides of the tin and prick the base with a fork.

To make the filling, put the butter and sugar in a bowl and beat until fluffy. Beat in the ground almonds and egg yolk and spoon into the pastry case. Arrange the sliced fruit over the filling. Mix the lemon juice and caster sugar together and brush over the top of the fruit filling.

Roll out the pastry trimmings and cut out leaf shapes and mark veins on. Brush the edge of the tart with milk, place the leaves round the edge and brush with milk. Bake for 30 minutes, or until the pastry is golden and the fruit is tender and golden. Serve with crème fraîche.

Almond & Pine Nut Tart

SERVES 6

250 g/9 oz ready-made sweet
   shortcrust pastry
75 g/3 oz blanched almonds
75 g/3 oz caster sugar
pinch salt
2 medium eggs

1 tsp vanilla extract
2–3 drops almond extract
125 g/4 oz unsalted
   butter, softened
2 tbsp flour
½ tsp baking powder

3–4 tbsp raspberry jam
50 g/2 oz pine nuts
icing sugar, to decorate
whipped cream, to serve

Preheat the oven to 200˚C/400˚F/Gas Mark 6. Roll out the pastry and use to line a 23 cm/9 inch fluted flan tin. Chill in the refrigerator for 10 minutes, then line with greaseproof paper and baking beans and bake blind in the preheated oven for 10 minutes. Remove the paper and beans and bake for a further 10–12 minutes until cooked. Leave to cool. Reduce the temperature to 190˚C/375˚F/Gas Mark 5.

Grind the almonds in a food processor until fine. Add the sugar, salt, eggs, vanilla and almond extract and blend. Add the butter, flour and baking powder and blend until smooth.

Spread a thick layer of the raspberry jam over the cooled pastry case, then pour in the almond filling. Sprinkle the pine nuts evenly over the top and bake for 30 minutes until firm and browned.

Remove the tart from the oven and leave to cool. Dust generously with icing sugar and serve cut into wedges with whipped cream.

Lattice Treacle Tart

SERVES 4

For the pastry:
175 g/6 oz plain flour
40 g/1½ oz butter
40 g/1½ oz white vegetable fat

For the filling:
225 g/8 oz golden syrup
finely grated zest and juice
of 1 lemon

75 g/3 oz fresh white
breadcrumbs
1 small egg, beaten

Preheat the oven to 190°C/375°F/Gas Mark 5. Make the pastry by placing the flour, butter and white vegetable fat in a food processor. Blend in short sharp bursts until the mixture resembles fine breadcrumbs. Remove from the processor and place on a pastry board or in a large bowl.

Stir in enough cold water to make a dough and knead in a large bowl or on a floured surface until smooth and pliable.

Roll out the pastry and use to line a 20.5 cm/8 inch loose-bottomed fluted flan dish or tin. Reserve the pastry trimmings for decoration. Chill for 30 minutes.

Meanwhile, to make the filling, place the golden syrup in a saucepan and warm gently with the lemon zest and juice. Tip the breadcrumbs into the pastry case and pour the syrup mixture over the top.

Roll the pastry trimmings out on a lightly floured surface and cut into 6–8 thin strips. Lightly dampen the pastry edge of the tart, then place the strips across the filling in a lattice pattern. Brush the ends of the strips with water and seal to the edge of the tart. Brush a little beaten egg over the pastry and bake in the preheated oven for 25 minutes, or until the filling is just set. Serve hot or cold.

Iced Bakewell Tart

CUTS INTO 8 SLICES

For the rich pastry:
175 g/6 oz plain flour
pinch salt
65 g/2½ oz butter, cut into
    small pieces
50 g/2 oz white vegetable fat,
    cut into small pieces
2 small egg yolks, beaten

For the filling:
125 g/4 oz butter, melted
125 g/4 oz caster sugar
125 g/4 oz ground almonds
2 large eggs, beaten
few drops almond extract
2 tbsp seedless
    raspberry jam

For the icing:
125 g/4 oz icing sugar, sifted
6–8 tsp fresh lemon juice
25 g/1 oz toasted
    flaked almonds

Preheat the oven to 200°C/400°F/Gas Mark 6. Place the flour and salt in a bowl and rub in the butter and vegetable fat until the mixture resembles breadcrumbs. Alternatively, blend quickly, in short bursts in a food processor.

Add the eggs with sufficient water to make a soft, pliable dough. Knead lightly on a floured board, then chill in the refrigerator for about 30 minutes. Roll out the pastry and use to line a 23 cm/9 inch loose-bottomed flan tin.

For the filling, mix together the melted butter, sugar, almonds and beaten eggs and add a few drops of almond extract. Spread the base of the pastry case with the raspberry jam and spoon the egg mixture over the top. Bake in the preheated oven for about 30 minutes until the filling is firm and golden brown. Remove from the oven and allow to cool completely.

When the tart is cold make the icing by mixing together the icing sugar and lemon juice, a little at a time, until the icing is smooth and of a spreadable consistency. Spread the icing over the tart, leave to set for 2–3 minutes and sprinkle with the almonds. Chill in the refrigerator for about 10 minutes before serving.

Chocolate Pecan Pie

225 g/8 oz prepared
   shortcrust pastry
   (*see* page 27)
200 g/7 oz pecan halves

125 g/4 oz dark
   chocolate, chopped
25 g/1 oz butter, diced
3 medium eggs

125 g/4 oz light brown sugar
175 ml/6 fl oz golden syrup
2 tsp vanilla extract
vanilla ice cream, to serve

Preheat the oven to 180°C/350°F/Gas Mark 4, 10 minutes before baking. Roll the prepared pastry out on a lightly floured surface and use to line a 25.5 cm/10 inch pie plate. Roll the trimmings out and use to make a decorative edge around the pie, then chill in the refrigerator for 1 hour.

Reserve about 60 perfect pecan halves, or enough to cover the top of the pie, then coarsely chop the remainder and reserve. Melt the chocolate and butter in a small saucepan over a low heat, or in the microwave, and reserve.

Beat the eggs and brush the base and sides of the pastry with a little of the beaten egg. Beat the sugar, golden syrup and vanilla extract into the beaten eggs. Add the pecans, then beat in the chocolate mixture.

Pour the filling into the pastry case and arrange the reserved pecan halves in concentric circles over the top. Bake in the preheated oven for 45–55 minutes until the filling is well risen and just set. If the pastry edge begins to brown too quickly, cover with strips of kitchen foil. Remove from the oven and leave to cool a little before serving warm or cold with ice cream.

Chocolate Apricot Linzer Torte

**CUTS INTO
10-12 SLICES**

**For the chocolate
almond pastry:**
75 g/3 oz whole
blanched almonds
125 g/4 oz caster sugar
215 g/7½ oz plain flour
2 tbsp cocoa powder

1 tsp ground cinnamon
½ tsp salt
grated zest of 1 orange
225 g/8 oz unsalted
butter, softened
2–3 tbsp iced water

For the filling:
350 g/12 oz apricot jam
75 g/3 oz milk chocolate,
chopped
icing sugar, for dusting

Preheat the oven to 190°C/375°F/Gas Mark 5, 10 minutes before baking. Lightly oil a 28 cm/11 inch flan tin. Place the almonds and half the sugar into a food processor and blend until finely ground. Add the remaining sugar, flour, cocoa powder, cinnamon, salt and orange zest and blend again. Add the diced butter and blend in short bursts to form coarse crumbs. Add the water 1 tablespoon at a time until the mixture starts to come together. Turn onto a lightly floured surface and knead lightly, roll out, then, using your fingertips, press half the dough onto the base and sides of the tin. Prick the base with a fork and chill in the refrigerator for 30 minutes. Roll out the remaining dough between two pieces of clingfilm to a 28–30.5 cm/11–12 inch round. Slide the round onto a baking sheet and chill in the refrigerator for 30 minutes.

For the filling, spread the apricot jam evenly over the chilled pastry base and sprinkle with the chopped chocolate.

Slide the dough round onto a lightly floured surface and peel off the top layer of clingfilm. Using a straight edge, cut the round into 1 cm/½ inch strips; allow to soften until slightly flexible. Place half the strips, about 1 cm/½ inch apart, to create a lattice pattern. Press down on each side of each crossing to accentuate the effect. Press the ends of the strips to the edge, cutting off any excess. Bake in the preheated oven for 35 minutes, or until cooked. Leave to cool before dusting with icing sugar and serve cut into slices.

Caramelised Chocolate Tartlets

SERVES 6

350 g/12 oz ready-made
   shortcrust pastry,
   thawed if frozen
150 ml/¼ pint coconut milk
40 g/1½ oz demerara sugar
50 g/2 oz dark
   chocolate, melted

1 medium egg, beaten
few drops vanilla extract
1 small mango, peeled,
   stoned and sliced
1 small papaya, peeled,
   deseeded and chopped
1 star fruit, sliced

1 kiwi, peeled and sliced, or
   use fruits of your choice

Preheat the oven to 200°C/400°F/Gas Mark 6, 15 minutes before baking. Lightly oil six individual tartlet tins. Roll out the ready-made pastry on a lightly floured surface and use to line the oiled tins. Prick the bases and sides with a fork and line with nonstick baking parchment and baking beans. Chill for 30 minutes in the refrigerator before baking blind in the preheated oven for 10 minutes, then remove from the oven and discard the baking beans and the baking parchment.

Reduce the oven temperature to 180°C/350°F/Gas Mark 4. Heat the coconut milk and 15 g/½ oz of the sugar in a heavy-based saucepan, stirring constantly, until the sugar has dissolved. Remove the saucepan from the heat and leave to cool.

Stir the melted chocolate, the beaten egg and the vanilla extract into the cooled coconut milk. Stir until well mixed, then strain into the cooked pastry cases. Place on a baking sheet and bake in the oven for 25 minutes, or until set. Remove and leave for at least 30 minutes or until cool, then chill in the refrigerator for 1 hour or until the filling is firm.

Preheat the grill, then arrange the fruits in a decorative pattern on the top of each tartlet. Sprinkle with the remaining demerara sugar and place the tartlets in the grill pan. Grill for 2 minutes, or until the sugar bubbles and browns. Turn the tartlets if necessary and take care not to burn the sugar. Remove from the grill and leave to cool before serving.

Chocolate Fruit Pizza

SERVES 8

1 quantity chocolate shortcrust
    pastry (*see* page 27)
2 tbsp chocolate spread
1 small peach, very
    thinly sliced
1 small nectarine, very
    thinly sliced

150 g/5 oz strawberries,
    halved or quartered
75 g/3 oz raspberries
75 g/3 oz blueberries
75 g/3 oz dark chocolate,
    coarsely chopped
1 tbsp butter, melted

2 tbsp granulated sugar
75 g/3 oz white chocolate,
    chopped
1 tbsp hazelnuts, toasted
    and chopped
fresh mint sprigs,
    to decorate

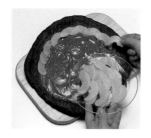

Preheat the oven to 200°C/400°F/Gas Mark 6, 15 minutes before baking. Lightly oil a large baking sheet. Roll the prepared pastry out to a 23 cm/9 inch round and place the pastry round onto the baking sheet and crimp the edges. Using a fork, prick the base all over and chill in the refrigerator for 30 minutes.

Line the pastry with foil and weigh down with an ovenproof flat dinner plate or base of a large flan tin and bake blind in the preheated oven until the edges begin to colour. Remove from the oven and discard the weight and foil.

Carefully spread the chocolate spread over the pizza base and arrange the peach and nectarine slices around the outside edge in overlapping circles. Toss the berries with the plain chocolate and arrange in the centre. Drizzle with the melted butter and sprinkle with the sugar.

Bake in the preheated oven for 10–12 minutes until the fruit begins to soften. Transfer the pizza to a wire rack. Sprinkle the white chocolate and hazelnuts over the surface and return to the oven for 1 minute, or until the chocolate begins to soften. If the pastry starts to darken too much, cover the edge with strips of foil. Remove to a wire rack and leave to cool. Decorate with sprigs of fresh mint and serve warm.

Chocolate Lemon Tartlets

MAKES 10

1 quantity chocolate shortcrust
    pastry (*see* page 27)
175 ml/6 fl oz double cream
175 g/6 oz dark
    chocolate, chopped
2 tbsp butter, diced

1 tsp vanilla essenceextract
350 g/12 oz lemon curd
225 ml/8 fl oz ready-made
    custard
225 ml/8 fl oz single cream
½ –1 tsp almond extract

To decorate:
grated chocolate
toasted flaked almonds

Preheat the oven to 200°C/400°F/Gas Mark 6, 15 minutes before baking. Roll the prepared pastry out on a lightly floured surface and use to line 10 x 7.5 cm/3 inch tartlet tins. Place a small piece of crumpled foil in each and bake blind in the preheated oven for 12 minutes. Remove from the oven and leave to cool.

Bring the cream to the boil, then remove from the heat and add the chocolate all at once. Stir until smooth and melted. Beat in the butter and vanilla extract and pour into the tartlets and leave to cool.

Beat the lemon curd until soft and spoon a thick layer over the chocolate in each tartlet, spreading gently to the edges. Do not chill in the refrigerator or the chocolate will be too firm.

Place the prepared custard sauce into a large bowl and gradually whisk in the cream and almond extract until the custard is smooth and runny.

To serve, spoon a little custard onto a plate and place a tartlet in the centre. Sprinkle with grated chocolate and almonds, then serve.

Chocolate Pecan Angel Pie

**CUTS INTO
8-10 SLICES**

4 large egg whites
¼ tsp cream of tartar
225 g/8 oz caster sugar
3 tsp vanilla extract
100 g/3½ oz pecans, lightly
   toasted and chopped

75 g/3 oz dark
   chocolate chips
150 ml/¼ pint double cream
150 g/5 oz white
   chocolate, grated

To decorate:
fresh raspberries
dark chocolate curls
few fresh mint sprigs

Preheat the oven to 110°C/225°F/Gas Mark ¼, 5 minutes before baking. Lightly oil a 23 cm/9 inch pie plate.

Using an electric mixer, whisk the egg whites and cream of tartar on a low speed until foamy, then increase the speed and beat until soft peaks form. Gradually beat in the sugar, 1 tablespoon at a time, beating well after each addition, until stiff glossy peaks form and the sugar is completely dissolved. (Test by rubbing a bit of meringue between your fingers – if gritty, continue beating.) This will take about 15 minutes. Beat in 2 teaspoons of the vanilla extract, then fold in the nuts and the chocolate chips.

Spread the meringue evenly in the pie plate, making a shallow well in the centre and slightly building up the sides. Bake in the preheated oven for 1–1¼ hours until a golden creamy colour. Lower the oven temperature if the meringue colours too quickly. Turn the oven off, but do not remove the meringue. Leave the oven door ajar (about 5 cm/2 inches) for about 1 hour. Transfer to a wire rack until cold.

Pour the double cream into a small saucepan and bring to the boil. Remove from the heat, add the grated white chocolate and stir until melted. Add the remaining vanilla extract and leave to cool, then whip until thick. Spoon the white chocolate cream into the pie shell, piling it high and swirling. Decorate with fresh raspberries and chocolate curls. Chill in the refrigerator for 2 hours before serving. When ready to serve, add sprigs of mint and cut into slices.

Bread & Butter Pudding

SERVES 4–6

2–3 tbsp unsalted
   butter, softened
4–6 slices white bread
75 g/3 oz mixed dried fruits
25 g/1 oz caster sugar, plus
   extra for sprinkling

2 medium eggs
450 ml/¾ pint semi-skimmed
   milk, warmed
freshly grated nutmeg
freshly made custard,
   to serve

Preheat the oven to 180°C/350°F/Gas Mark 4, 10 minutes before cooking. Lightly butter a 1.1 litre/2 pint ovenproof dish. Butter the bread and cut into quarters. Arrange half the bread in the dish and scatter over two-thirds of the dried fruit and sugar. Repeat the layering, finishing with the dried fruits.

Beat the eggs and milk together and pour over the bread and butter. Leave to stand for 30 minutes.

Sprinkle with the remaining sugar and a little nutmeg and carefully place in the oven. Cook for 40 minutes, or until the pudding has lightly set and the top is golden.

Remove and sprinkle with a little extra sugar, if liked. Serve with freshly made custard.

Chocolate Brioche Bake

SERVES 6

200 g/7 oz dark chocolate, broken into pieces
75 g/3 oz unsalted butter
225 g/8 oz brioche, sliced

1 tsp pure orange oil, or 1 tbsp grated orange zest
½ tsp freshly grated nutmeg
3 medium eggs, beaten

25 g/1 oz golden caster sugar
600 ml/1 pint milk
cocoa powder and icing sugar, for dusting

Preheat the oven to 180°C/350°F/Gas Mark 4, 10 minutes before baking. Lightly oil or butter a 1.7 litre/3 pint ovenproof dish. Melt the chocolate with 25 g/1 oz of the butter in a heatproof bowl set over a saucepan of simmering water. Stir until smooth.

Arrange half of the sliced brioche in the ovenproof dish, overlapping the slices slightly, then pour over half of the melted chocolate. Repeat the layers, finishing with a layer of chocolate.

Melt the remaining butter in a saucepan. Remove from the heat and stir in the orange oil or zest, the nutmeg and the beaten eggs. Continuing to stir, add the sugar and finally the milk. Beat thoroughly and pour over the brioche. Leave to stand for 30 minutes before baking.

Bake on the centre shelf in the preheated oven for 45 minutes, or until the custard is set and the topping is golden brown. Leave to stand for 5 minutes, then dust with cocoa powder and icing sugar. Serve warm.

Peach & Chocolate Bake

SERVES 6

200 g/7 oz dark chocolate
125 g/4 oz unsalted butter
4 medium eggs, separated
125 g/4 oz caster sugar
425 g can peach
   slices, drained

½ tsp ground cinnamon
1 tbsp icing sugar, sifted,
   to decorate
crème fraîche, to serve

Preheat the oven to 170°C/325°F/Gas Mark 3, 10 minutes before baking. Lightly oil a 1.7 litre/3 pint ovenproof dish.

Break the chocolate and butter into small pieces and place in a small heatproof bowl set over a saucepan of gently simmering water. Ensure the water is not touching the base of the bowl and leave to melt. Remove the bowl from the heat and stir until smooth.

Whisk the egg yolks with the sugar until very thick and creamy, then stir the melted chocolate and butter into the whisked egg yolk mixture and mix together lightly.

Place the egg whites in a clean, grease-free bowl and whisk until stiff, then fold 2 tablespoons of the whisked egg whites into the chocolate mixture. Mix well, then add the remaining egg whites and fold in very lightly.

Fold the peach slices and the cinnamon into the mixture, then spoon the mixture into the prepared dish. Do not level the mixture, leave a little uneven.

Bake in the preheated oven for 35–40 minutes until well risen and just firm to the touch. Sprinkle the bake with the icing sugar and serve immediately with spoonfuls of crème fraîche.

Luxury Mince Pies

275 g/10 oz plain flour
25 g/1 oz ground almonds
175 g/6 oz butter, diced
75 g/3 oz icing sugar
zest of 1 lemon, finely grated

1 egg yolk
3 tbsp milk

For the filling:
225 g/8 oz mincemeat

1 tbsp dark rum or
   orange juice
zest of 1 orange, finely grated
75 g/3 oz dried cranberries
icing sugar, for dusting

Sift the flour and ground almonds into a bowl or a food processor and add the butter. Rub in, or process, until the mixture resembles fine crumbs. Sift in the icing sugar and stir in the lemon zest. Whisk the egg yolk and milk together in a separate bowl and stir into the mixture until a soft dough forms. Wrap the pastry in clingfilm and chill for 30 minutes.

Preheat the oven to 200°C/400°F/Gas Mark 6. Grease two 12-hole patty tins. Roll out the pastry on a lightly floured surface to 3 mm/⅛ inch thickness. Cut out 20 rounds using a 7.5 cm/3 inch fluted round pastry cutter. Re-roll the trimmings into thin strips.

Mix the filling ingredients together in a bowl. Place 1 tablespoon of the filling in each pastry case, then dampen the edges of each case with a little water. Put four strips of pastry over the top of each case to form a lattice.

Bake for 10–15 minutes until the pastry is crisp. Dust with icing sugar and serve hot or cold.

Puff Pastry Jalousie

SERVES 6–8

2 large dessert apples,
   peeled and cored
4 tbsp mincemeat
zest of 1 orange, finely grated

1 tbsp orange marmalade
350 g/12 oz puff pastry
1 medium egg, beaten
caster sugar, for sprinkling

custard or double cream,
   to serve

Preheat the oven to 200°C/400°F/Gas Mark 6 and grease a large baking sheet. Grate the apples coarsely, then mix together with the mincemeat, orange zest and the marmalade, then reserve.

Place the pastry on a lightly floured surface and cut it in half. Roll each piece into an 18 x 25 cm/7 x 10 inch rectangle. Place one of the rectangles on the baking sheet.

Spoon the filling down the middle, leaving a 2.5 cm/1 inch edge all round. Brush the pastry edges with the beaten egg. Score thin lines across the middle of the remaining pastry rectangle right through the pastry, leaving a plain narrow 2.5 cm/1 inch rim all round. Lift the scored pastry on top of the filling and press the edges together to seal. Place on the baking sheet.

Brush the pastry with the beaten egg and bake for about 30 minutes until golden and crisp. Sprinkle generously with caster sugar and return to the oven for 5 minutes. Serve hot with custard or double cream.

Baked Apple Dumplings

SERVES 4

225 g/8 oz self-raising flour
¼ tsp salt
125 g/4 oz shredded suet

4 medium cooking apples
4–6 tsp luxury mincemeat
1 medium egg white, beaten

2 tsp caster sugar
custard or vanilla sauce,
  to serve

Preheat the oven to 200°C/400°F/Gas Mark 6. Lightly oil a baking tray. Place the flour and salt in a bowl and stir in the suet. Add just enough water to the mixture to mix to a soft but not sticky dough, using the fingertips.

Turn the dough onto a lightly floured board and knead lightly into a ball. Divide the dough into 4 pieces and roll out each piece into a thin square, large enough to encase the apples.

Peel and core the apples and place 1 apple in the centre of each square of pastry. Fill the centre of the apple with mincemeat, brush the edges of each pastry square with water and draw the corners up to meet over each apple. Press the edges of the pastry firmly together and decorate with pastry leaves and shapes made from the extra pastry trimmings.

Place the apples on the prepared baking tray, brush with the egg white and sprinkle with the sugar. Bake in the preheated oven for 30 minutes, or until golden and the pastry and apples are cooked. Serve the dumplings hot with the custard or vanilla sauce.

Eve's Pudding

SERVES 6

450 g/1 lb cooking apples	125 g/4 oz caster sugar	125 g/4 oz self-raising flour
175 g/6 oz blackberries	125 g/4 oz butter	1 tbsp icing sugar
75 g/3 oz demerara sugar	few drops vanilla extract	ready-made custard, to serve
grated zest of 1 lemon	2 medium eggs, beaten	

Preheat the oven to 180°C/350°F/Gas Mark 4. Oil a 1.1 litre/2 pint baking dish.

Peel, core and slice the apples and place a layer in the base of the prepared dish. Sprinkle over some of the blackberries, a little demerara sugar and some lemon zest.

Continue to layer the apple and blackberries in this way until all the ingredients have been used.

Cream the sugar and butter together until light and fluffy. Beat in the vanilla extract and then the eggs a little at a time, adding a spoonful of flour after each addition. Fold in the extra flour with a metal spoon or rubber spatula and mix well.

Spread the sponge mixture over the top of the fruit and level with the back of a spoon. Place the dish on a baking sheet and bake in the preheated oven for 35–40 minutes until well risen and golden brown. (To test if the pudding is cooked, press the sponge lightly with a clean finger – if it springs back, the sponge is cooked.)

Dust the pudding with a little icing sugar and serve immediately with the custard.

Golden Castle Pudding

SERVES 4-6

125 g/4 oz butter
125 g/4 oz caster sugar
few drops vanilla extract

2 medium eggs, beaten
125 g/4 oz self-raising flour
4 tbsp golden syrup

crème fraîche or ready-made
custard, to serve

Preheat the oven to 180°C/350°F/Gas Mark 4. Lightly oil 4–6 individual pudding bowls and place a small circle of lightly oiled nonstick baking or greaseproof paper in the base of each.

Place the butter and caster sugar in a large bowl, then beat together until the mixture is pale and creamy. Stir in the vanilla extract and gradually add the beaten eggs, a little at a time. Add a tablespoon of flour after each addition of egg and beat well.

When the mixture is smooth, add the remaining flour and fold in gently. Add a tablespoon of water and mix to form a soft mixture that will drop easily off a spoon.

Spoon enough mixture into each basin to come halfway up the tin, allowing enough space for the puddings to rise. Place on a baking sheet and bake in the preheated oven for about 25 minutes until firm and golden brown.

Allow the puddings to stand for 5 minutes. Discard the paper circles and turn out onto individual serving plates.

Warm the golden syrup in a small saucepan and pour a little over each pudding. Serve hot with the crème fraîche or custard.

College Pudding

SERVES 4

125 g/4 oz shredded suet
125 g/4 oz fresh white
   breadcrumbs
50 g/2 oz sultanas

50 g/2 oz seedless raisins
½ tsp ground cinnamon
¼ tsp freshly grated nutmeg
¼ tsp mixed spice

50 g/2 oz caster sugar
½ tsp baking powder
2 medium eggs, beaten
orange zest, to garnish

Preheat the oven to 180°C/350°F/Gas Mark 4. Lightly oil an ovenproof 900 ml/1½ pint pudding basin and place a small circle of greaseproof paper in the base.

Mix the shredded suet and breadcrumbs together and rub lightly together with the fingertips to remove any lumps.

Stir in the dried fruit, spices, sugar and baking powder. Add the eggs and beat lightly together until the mixture is well blended and the fruit is evenly distributed.

Spoon the mixture into the prepared pudding basin and level the surface. Place on a baking tray and cover lightly with some greaseproof paper.

Bake in the preheated oven for 20 minutes, then remove the paper and continue to bake for a further 10–15 minutes until the top is firm.

When the pudding is cooked, remove from the oven and carefully turn out onto a warmed serving dish. Decorate with the orange zest and serve immediately.

Basic Breads
& Scones

Quick Brown Bread

**MAKES TWO
450 G/1 LB LOAVES**

700 g/1½ lb strong
   wholemeal flour
2 tsp salt
½ tsp caster sugar
7 g oz sachet fast-action
   dried yeast
450 ml/¾ pint warm water

To finish:
beaten egg, to glaze
1 tbsp plain white flour,
   to dust

**For onion and caraway
   seed rolls:**
1 small onion, peeled and
   finely chopped
1 tbsp olive oil
2 tbsp caraway seeds
milk, to glaze

Preheat the oven to 200°C/400°F/Gas Mark 6, 15 minutes before baking. Oil two 450 g/1 lb loaf tins. Sift the flour, salt and sugar into a large bowl, adding the bran remaining in the sieve. Stir in the yeast, then make a well in the centre.

Pour the warm water into the dry ingredients and mix to form a soft dough, adding a little more water if needed. Knead on a lightly floured surface for 10 minutes, or until smooth and elastic. Divide in half, shape into two oblongs and place in the tins. Cover with oiled clingfilm and leave in a warm place for 40 minutes, or until risen to the tops of the tins.

Glaze one loaf with the beaten egg and dust the other loaf generously with the plain flour. Bake the loaves in the preheated oven for 35 minutes, or until well risen and lightly browned. Turn out of the tins and return to the oven for 5 minutes to crisp the sides. Cool on a wire rack.

For the onion and caraway seed rolls, gently fry the onion in the oil until soft. Reserve until the onion is cool, then stir into the dry ingredients with 1 tablespoon of the caraway seeds. Make the dough as before. Divide the dough into 16 pieces and shape into rolls. Put on two oiled baking trays, cover with oiled clingfilm and prove for 30 minutes. Glaze the rolls with milk and sprinkle with the rest of the seeds. Bake for 25–30 minutes, cool on a wire rack and serve.

Classic White Loaf

700 g/1½ lb strong
   white flour
1 tbsp salt
25 g/1 oz butter, cubed
1 tsp caster sugar
2 tsp fast-action dried yeast
150 ml/¼ pint milk

300 ml/½ pint warm water
1 tbsp plain flour, to dredge

**For a light wholemeal
   variation:**
450 g/1 lb strong
   wholemeal flour

225 g/8 oz strong white flour
beaten egg, to glaze
1 tbsp kibbled wheat,
   to finish

Preheat the oven to 220°C/425°F/Gas Mark 7, 15 minutes before baking. Oil and line the base of a 900 g/2 lb loaf tin with greaseproof paper. Sift the flour and salt into a large bowl. Rub in the butter, then stir in the sugar and yeast. Make a well in the centre.

Add the milk and the warm water to the dry ingredients. Mix to a soft dough, adding a little more water if needed. Turn out the dough and knead on a lightly floured surface for 10 minutes, or until smooth and elastic.

Place the dough in an oiled bowl, cover with clingfilm or a clean tea towel and leave in a warm place to rise for 1 hour, or until doubled in size. Knead again for a minute or two to knock out the air. Shape the dough into an oblong and place in the prepared tin. Cover with oiled clingfilm and leave to rise for a further 30 minutes, or until the dough reaches the top of the tin. Dredge the top of the loaf with flour, or brush with the egg glaze and scatter with kibbled wheat if making the wholemeal version. Bake the loaf on the middle shelf of the preheated oven for 15 minutes.

Turn down the oven to 200°C/400°F/Gas Mark 6. Bake the loaf for a further 20–25 minutes until well risen and hollow-sounding when tapped underneath. Turn out, cool on a wire rack and serve.

Multigrain Bread

350 g/12 oz strong white flour
2 tsp salt
225 g/8 oz strong
   granary flour

125 g/4 oz rye flour
25 g/1 oz butter, diced
2 tsp fast-action dried yeast
25 g/1 oz rolled oats

2 tbsp sunflower seeds
1 tbsp malt extract
450 ml/¾ pint warm water
1 medium egg, beaten

Preheat the oven to 220°C/425°F/Gas Mark 7, 15 minutes before baking. Sift the white flour and salt into a large bowl. Stir in the granary and rye flours, then rub in the butter until the mixture resembles breadcrumbs. Stir in the yeast, oats and seeds and make a well in the centre.

Stir the malt extract into the warm water until dissolved. Add the malt water to the dry ingredients. Mix to a soft dough. Turn the dough out onto a lightly floured surface and knead for 10 minutes, or until smooth and elastic.

Put in an oiled bowl, cover with clingfilm and leave to rise in a warm place for 1½ hours, or until doubled in size. Turn out and knead again for a minute or two to knock out the air. Shape into an oval loaf about 30.5 cm/12 inches long and place on a well-oiled baking sheet. Cover with oiled clingfilm and leave to rise for 40 minutes, or until doubled in size.

Brush the loaf with beaten egg and bake in the preheated oven for 35–45 minutes until the bread is well risen, browned and sounds hollow when the base is tapped. Leave to cool on a wire rack, then serve.

Wholemeal Walnut Bread

**MAKES TWO
350 G/12 OZ LOAVES**

700 g/1½ lb strong wholemeal bread flour	7 g sachet fast-action dried yeast	2 tbsp walnut oil
1½ tsp sea salt	450 ml/¾ pint lukewarm water	1 tbsp clear honey
		125 g/4 oz walnuts

Place the flour, salt and yeast in a large bowl and stir together. Make a well in the middle and pour in the lukewarm water, the walnut oil and the honey. Gradually work the flour into the liquid until it comes together to make a ball of dough.

Place the dough on a lightly floured surface and knead for about 10 minutes until it is smooth, soft and stretchy, or place the dough in a tabletop mixer fitted with a dough hook and knead for 5 minutes until smooth.

Preheat a grill and line a baking sheet with foil. Place the walnuts on the baking sheet and grill for a few minutes to toast them. Cool the nuts, then chop them coarsely. Knead the chopped walnuts into the dough. Divide the dough in half and then shape into two balls. Dust the top of the bread lightly with flour and cut slashes into the top with a sharp knife to a depth of about 2 cm/¾ inch. Oil a large baking sheet and place the dough on it. Cover with oiled clingfilm and leave in a warm place for about 40 minutes to 1 hour until doubled in size.

Preheat the oven to 200°C/400°F/Gas Mark 6. Discard the clingfilm and place the dough in the oven. Bake for 35 minutes until golden. Tap the bread, which should sound hollow when it is cooked. If it sounds heavy, bake it for a few more minutes. Place on a wire rack to cool.

Irish Soda Bread

400 g/14 oz plain white flour,
    plus 1 tbsp for dusting
1 tsp salt
2 tsp bicarbonate of soda
15 g/½ oz butter

50 g/2 oz coarse oatmeal
1 tsp clear honey
300 ml/½ pint buttermilk
2 tbsp milk

For a wholemeal variation:
400 g/14 oz plain wholemeal
    flour, plus 1 tbsp
    for dusting
1 tbsp milk

Preheat the oven to 200°C/400°F/Gas Mark 6, 15 minutes before baking. Sift the flour, salt and bicarbonate of soda into a large bowl. Rub in the butter until the mixture resembles fine breadcrumbs. Stir in the oatmeal and make a well in the centre.

Mix the honey, buttermilk and milk together and add to the dry ingredients. Mix to a soft dough.

Knead the dough on a lightly floured surface for 2–3 minutes until the dough is smooth. Shape into a 20.5 cm/8 inch round and place on an oiled baking sheet.

Thickly dust the top of the bread with flour. Using a sharp knife, cut a deep cross on top, going about halfway through the loaf.

Bake on the middle shelf of the preheated oven for 30–35 minutes until the bread is slightly risen, golden and sounds hollow when tapped underneath. Cool on a wire rack. Eat on the day of making.

For a wholemeal soda bread, use all wholemeal flour instead of the white flour and add an extra tablespoon of milk when mixing together. Dust the top with wholemeal flour and bake.

Soft Dinner Rolls

MAKES 16

		To glaze and finish:
50 g/2 oz butter	1½ tsp salt	**To glaze and finish:**
1 tbsp caster sugar	2 tsp fast-action	2 tbsp milk
225 ml/8 fl oz milk	dried yeast	1 tsp sea salt
550 g/1¼ lb strong white flour	2 medium eggs, beaten	2 tsp poppy seeds

Preheat the oven to 220°C/425°F/Gas Mark 7, 15 minutes before baking. Gently heat the butter, sugar and milk in a saucepan until the butter has melted and the sugar has dissolved. Cool until tepid. Sift the flour and salt into a bowl, stir in the yeast and make a well in the centre. Reserve 1 tablespoon of the beaten eggs. Add the rest to the dry ingredients with the milk mixture. Mix to form a soft dough.

Knead the dough on a lightly floured surface for 10 minutes until smooth and elastic. Put in an oiled bowl, cover with clingfilm and leave in a warm place to rise for 1 hour, or until doubled in size. Knead again for a minute or two, then divide into 16 pieces. Shape into plaits, snails, clover leaves and cottage buns (as illustrated). Place on two oiled baking sheets, cover with oiled clingfilm and leave to rise for 30 minutes until doubled in size.

Mix the reserved beaten egg with the milk and brush over the rolls. Sprinkle some with sea salt, others with poppy seeds and leave some plain. Bake in the preheated oven for about 20 minutes until golden and hollow-sounding when tapped underneath. Transfer to a wire rack. Cover with a clean tea towel while cooling to keep the rolls soft, and serve.

Tomato & Basil Rolls

**MAKES 10
LARGE ROLLS**

575 g/1¼ lb strong white bread flour	5 tbsp olive oil	25 g/1 oz chopped fresh basil
2 tsp salt	300 ml/½ pint lukewarm water	25 g/1 oz Parmesan cheese, finely grated
7 g sachet fast-action dried yeast	2 tbsp tomato purée	1 tbsp sea salt
	100 g/3½ oz soft sun-dried tomatoes, chopped	

Sift the flour and salt into a bowl and stir in the yeast. Add 4 tablespoons of the olive oil, the lukewarm water and the tomato purée and mix to a soft dough. Knead the dough by hand for 10 minutes, or place in a tabletop mixer fitted with a dough hook and knead for 5 minutes until smooth and elastic.

Return to the bowl and cover with oiled clingfilm. Leave in a warm place for about 1 hour until doubled in size. Turn the dough onto a floured surface and punch it to knock out all the air. Knead in the chopped tomatoes, basil and Parmesan cheese.

Cut the dough into 10 pieces. Roll each piece out into a ball and brush over the tops with the remaining 1 tablespoon olive oil. Make shallow diamond-shaped slashes across the top of each one with a sharp knife.

Cover the rolls with oiled clingfilm and leave for about 45 minutes until doubled in size. Preheat the oven to 220°C/425°F/Gas Mark 7, 10–15 minutes before baking. Discard the clingfilm and scatter the sea salt over the rolls. Bake for about 20 minutes until risen and golden and the rolls sound hollow when tapped. Leave to cool on a wire rack.

Sweet Potato Baps

MAKES 16

225 g/8 oz sweet potato
15 g/½ oz butter
freshly grated nutmeg
about 200 ml/7 fl oz milk
450 g/1 lb strong white flour

2 tsp salt
7 g sachet fast-action
  dried yeast
1 medium egg, beaten

To finish:
beaten egg, to glaze
1 tbsp rolled oats

Preheat the oven to 200°C/400°F/Gas Mark 6, 15 minutes before baking. Peel the sweet potato and cut into large chunks. Cook in a saucepan of boiling water for 12–15 minutes until tender. Drain well and mash with the butter and nutmeg. Stir in the milk, then leave until barely warm.

Sift the flour and salt into a large bowl. Stir in the yeast. Make a well in the centre. Add the mashed sweet potato and beaten egg and mix to a soft dough. Add a little more milk if needed, depending on the moisture in the sweet potato.

Turn out the dough onto a lightly floured surface and knead for about 10 minutes until smooth and elastic. Place in a lightly oiled bowl, cover with clingfilm and leave in a warm place to rise for about 1 hour until the dough doubles in size.

Turn out the dough and knead for a minute or two until smooth. Divide into 16 pieces, shape into rolls and place on a large oiled baking sheet. Cover with oiled clingfilm and leave to rise for 15 minutes.

Brush the rolls with beaten egg, then sprinkle half with rolled oats and leave the rest plain. Bake in the preheated oven for 12–15 minutes until well risen, lightly browned and sound hollow when the bases are tapped. Transfer to a wire rack and immediately cover with a clean tea towel to keep the crusts soft.

Poppy Seed Plait

MAKES 1 LOAF

500 g/1 lb 2 oz strong white bread flour	25 g/1 oz white vegetable fat	150 ml/¼ pint lukewarm water
2 tsp salt	7 g sachet fast-action dried yeast	1 medium egg, beaten
2 tsp caster sugar	150 ml /¼ pint milk	2 tbsp poppy seeds

Sift the flour and salt into a bowl and stir in the sugar. Cut the fat into small cubes and rub into the flour in the bowl until it forms fine crumbs. Stir in the yeast and add the milk and lukewarm water.

Mix to a soft dough. Place in a tabletop mixer fitted with a dough hook and knead for 5 minutes, or turn out onto a floured surface and knead by hand for about 10 minutes until smooth and elastic.

Return to the bowl and cover with oiled clingfilm. Leave in a warm place for about 1 hour until doubled in size. Discard the clingfilm, place the dough on a floured surface and knead it to knock out all the air.

Grease a baking sheet. Divide the dough into three equal pieces and roll each into a thin rope about 30 cm/12 inches long. Place the ropes side by side and plait them, starting from halfway down. Be careful not to stretch the dough. Join the ends and tuck underneath. Place the plaited loaf on the baking sheet. Cover with oiled clingfilm and leave to rise in a warm place for about 45 minutes until doubled in size.

Preheat the oven to 220°C/425°F/Gas Mark 7. Discard the clingfilm and brush the risen dough with the beaten egg. Sprinkle over the poppy seeds and bake for about 30 minutes or until golden. To test if the bread is cooked, tap the underside with your knuckles. It should sound hollow if the bread is done. Cool on a wire rack. Eat within 24 hours.

Rosemary & Olive Focaccia

700 g/1½ lb strong
   white flour
pinch salt
pinch caster sugar
7 g/¼ oz sachet fast-action
   dried yeast
2 tsp freshly chopped
   rosemary

450 ml/¾ pint warm water
3 tbsp olive oil
75 g/3 oz pitted black olives,
   roughly chopped
rosemary sprigs, to garnish

To finish:
3 tbsp olive oil

coarse sea salt
freshly ground black pepper

Preheat the oven to 200°C/400°F/Gas Mark 6, 15 minutes before baking. Sift the flour, salt and sugar into a large bowl. Stir in the yeast and rosemary. Make a well in the centre.

Pour in the warm water and the oil and mix to a soft dough. Turn out onto a lightly floured surface and knead for about 10 minutes until smooth and elastic.

Pat the olives dry on kitchen paper, then gently knead into the dough. Put in an oiled bowl, cover with clingfilm and leave to rise in a warm place for 1½ hours, or until doubled in size.

Turn out the dough and knead again for a minute or two. Divide in half and roll out each piece to a 25.5 cm/10 inch round. Transfer to oiled baking sheets, cover with oiled clingfilm and leave to rise for 30 minutes.

Using the fingertips, make deep dimples all over the dough. Drizzle with the oil and sprinkle with sea salt.

Bake in the preheated oven for 20–25 minutes until risen and golden. Cool on a wire rack and garnish with sprigs of rosemary. Grind over a little black pepper before serving.

Chapattis

MAKES 6

225 g/8 oz wholemeal flour
½ tsp salt
125 ml/4 fl oz warm water

Sift the flour and salt into a bowl, adding any bran left in the sieve. Add the water a little at a time and knead until a firm dough forms.

Replace the dough in the bowl and cover with a damp, clean cloth, such as a tea towel, and leave to rest for 20 minutes.

Divide the dough into 6 equal pieces and roll them out on a lightly floured surface into thin rounds about 15 cm/6 inches wide.

Preheat a heavy-based frying pan or a griddle pan until it is so hot that water will sizzle if a few drops are added.

Cook one chapatti at a time in the pan, pressing down until brown, then flip it over and cook it on the other side. Keep the breads warm, covered with a cloth, while you cook the remaining dough. Eat immediately, served with curry and rice.

Spicy Filled Naan Bread

400 g/14 oz strong white flour
1 tsp salt
1 tsp fast-action dried yeast
15 g/½ oz ghee or unsalted
    butter, melted
1 tsp clear honey
200 ml/7 fl oz warm water

For the filling:
25 g/1 oz ghee or
    unsalted butter
1 small onion, peeled and
    finely chopped
1 garlic clove, peeled
    and crushed

1 tsp ground coriander
1 tsp ground cumin
2 tsp grated fresh root ginger
pinch chilli powder
pinch ground cinnamon
salt and freshly ground
    black pepper

Preheat the oven to 230°C/450°F/Gas Mark 8, 15 minutes before baking and place a large baking sheet in to heat up. Sift the flour and salt into a large bowl. Stir in the yeast and make a well in the centre. Add the ghee or melted butter, honey and the warm water. Mix to a soft dough.

Knead the dough on a lightly floured surface until smooth and elastic. Put in a lightly oiled bowl, cover with clingfilm and leave to rise for 1 hour, or until doubled in size.

For the filling, melt the ghee or butter in a frying pan and gently cook the onion for about 5 minutes. Stir in the garlic and spices and season to taste with salt and pepper. Cook for a further 6–7 minutes until soft. Remove from the heat, stir in 1 tablespoon of water and leave to cool.

Briefly knead the dough, then divide into six pieces. Roll out each piece of dough to 12.5 cm/ 5 inch rounds. Spoon the filling onto one half of each round. Fold over and press the edges together to seal. Re-roll to shape into flat ovals, about 16 cm/6½ inches long. Cover with oiled clingfilm and leave to rise for about 15 minutes.

Transfer the breads to the hot baking sheet and cook in the preheated oven for 10–12 minutes until puffed up and lightly browned. Serve hot.

Hot Cross Buns

MAKES 12

500 g/1 lb 2 oz strong white
   bread flour
1 tsp salt
2 tsp mixed spice
50 g/2 oz soft light
   brown sugar

7 g sachet fast-action
   dried yeast
275 ml/9 fl oz milk
1 medium egg, beaten
50 g/2 oz butter, melted
   and cooled
225 g/8 oz mixed dried fruit

For the decoration:
1 medium egg, beaten
75 g/3 oz shortcrust pastry
50 g/2 oz caster sugar

Sift the flour, salt and spice into a bowl and then stir in the sugar and yeast. In a jug, whisk together the milk and the egg. Add the liquid to the flour in the bowl with the cooled melted butter and mix to a soft dough. Knead for 10 minutes by hand, or for 5 minutes using a tabletop mixer fitted with a dough hook, until smooth and elastic.

Knead in the fruit and then place the dough in a bowl. Cover it with oiled clingfilm. Leave in a warm place for about 1 hour until doubled in size. Butter a large 32 x 23 cm/12 x 9 inch baking tray or a roasting tin. Cut the dough into 12 chunks and roll each one into a ball. Place in the tray, leaving enough space for the buns to rise and spread out. Cover with the oiled clingfilm and leave for about 45 minutes until doubled in size.

Preheat the oven to 200°C/400°F/Gas Mark 6. Discard the clingfilm and brush the buns with the beaten egg. Roll the pastry into long thin strips. Place a pastry strip over and along the length of each bun, then place another strip in the opposite direction to make crosses. Repeat, topping all the buns with pastry crosses. Bake for 20–25 minutes until risen and golden.

Heat 2 tablespoons of water and add the caster sugar, continuing to heat gently until the sugar is completely dissolved. While still hot, turn the buns out of the tray and place on a wire rack. Brush the sugar glaze over the warm buns and leave to cool. These are best eaten on the day of baking. Split and toast any leftovers and serve with butter.

Traditional Oven Scones

225 g/8 oz self-raising flour
1 tsp baking powder
pinch salt
40 g/1½ oz butter, cubed
15 g/½ oz caster sugar

150 ml/¼ pint milk, plus
   1 tbsp for brushing
1 tbsp plain flour, to dust

**For a lemon and sultana
   scone variation:**
50 g/2 oz sultanas
finely grated zest of ½ lemon
beaten egg, to glaze

Preheat the oven to 220°C/425°F/Gas Mark 7, 15 minutes before baking. Sift the flour, baking powder and salt into a large bowl. Rub in the butter until the mixture resembles fine breadcrumbs. Stir in the sugar and mix in enough milk to give a fairly soft dough.

Knead the dough on a lightly floured surface for a few seconds until smooth. Roll out until 2 cm/¾ inch thick and stamp out 6.5 cm/2½ inch rounds with a floured plain cutter.

Place on an oiled baking sheet and brush the tops with milk (do not brush it over the sides or the scones will not rise properly). Dust with a little plain flour.

Bake in the preheated oven for 12–15 minutes until well risen and golden brown. Transfer to a wire rack and serve warm or leave to cool completely.

For lemon and sultana scones, stir in the sultanas and lemon zest with the sugar. Roll out until 2 cm/¾ inch thick and cut into 8 fingers, 10 x 2.5 cm/4 x 1 inch in size. Bake the scones as before.

Cheese–crusted Potato Scones

MAKES 6

200 g/7 oz self-raising flour
25 g/1 oz wholemeal flour
½ tsp salt
1½ tsp baking powder
25 g/1 oz butter, cubed
5 tbsp milk

175 g/6 oz cold
   mashed potato
freshly ground black pepper

To finish:
2 tbsp milk

40 g/1½ oz mature Cheddar
   cheese, finely grated
paprika, for dusting
basil sprig, to garnish

Preheat the oven to 220˚C/425˚F/Gas Mark 7, 15 minutes before baking. Sift the flours, salt and baking powder into a large bowl. Rub in the butter until the mixture resembles fine breadcrumbs.

Stir 4 tablespoons of the milk into the mashed potato and season with black pepper.

Add the dry ingredients to the potato mixture, mixing together with a fork and adding the remaining 1 tablespoon of milk if needed.

Knead the dough on a lightly floured surface for a few seconds until smooth. Roll out to a 15 cm/6 inch round and transfer to an oiled baking sheet. Mark the scone round into 6 wedges, cutting about halfway through with a small sharp knife. Brush with milk, then sprinkle with the cheese and a faint dusting of paprika. Bake on the middle shelf of the preheated oven for 15 minutes, or until well risen and golden brown.

Transfer to a wire rack and leave to cool for 5 minutes before breaking into wedges. Serve warm or leave to cool completely. Garnish with a sprig of basil and serve split and buttered.

Banana & Honey Tea Bread

2 large peeled bananas, about 225 g/8 oz	125 g/4 oz soft light brown sugar	225 g/8 oz wholemeal self-raising flour
1 tbsp fresh orange juice	125 g/4 oz honey	½ tsp ground cinnamon
125 g/4 oz soft margarine	2 medium eggs, beaten	75 g/3 oz sultanas

Preheat the oven to 180°C/350°F/Gas Mark 4. Grease a 900 g/2 lb loaf tin and line the base with a strip of nonstick baking parchment. Mash the bananas together in a large bowl with the orange juice.

Place the soft margarine, sugar and honey in the bowl and add the eggs. Sift in the flour and cinnamon, adding any bran left behind in the sieve. Beat everything together until light and fluffy and then fold in the sultanas.

Spoon the mixture into the prepared tin and smooth the top to make it level. Bake for about 1 hour until golden, well risen and a skewer inserted into the centre comes out clean.

Cool in the tin for 5 minutes, then turn out on a wire rack.

Fruity Apple Tea Bread

125 g/4 oz butter
125 g/4 oz soft light
  brown sugar
275 g/10 oz sultanas
150 ml/¼ pint apple juice
1 eating apple, peeled, cored
  and chopped

2 medium eggs, beaten
275 g/10 oz plain flour
½ tsp ground cinnamon
½ tsp ground ginger
2 tsp bicarbonate of soda
butter curls, to serve

To decorate:
1 eating apple, cored
  and sliced
1 tsp lemon juice
1 tbsp golden syrup, warmed

Preheat the oven to 180°C/350°F/Gas Mark 4. Oil and line the base of a 900 g/2 lb loaf tin with nonstick baking parchment.

Put the butter, sugar, sultanas and apple juice in a small saucepan. Heat gently, stirring occasionally, until the butter has melted. Tip into a mixing bowl and leave to cool.

Stir the chopped apple and beaten eggs into the cooled sultana mixture. Sift in the flour, spices and bicarbonate of soda and mix well.

Spoon into the prepared tin and level the top with the back of a spoon.

Toss the apple slices in lemon juice and arrange on top. Bake in the preheated oven for 50 minutes, then cover with foil to prevent the top from browning too much, and bake for a further 30–35 minutes until a skewer inserted into the centre comes out clean.

Brush the top with golden syrup then leave to cool in the tin before turning out onto a wire rack. Leave until cold. Remove the lining paper, cut into thick slices and serve with curls of butter.

Savoury Baking

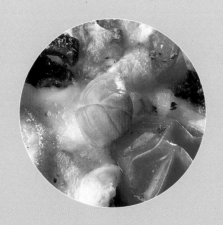

Sausage Rolls

MAKES 12

175 g/6 oz plain flour
pinch salt
40 g/1½ oz butter or
   block margarine
40 g/1½ oz white vegetable fat
1 egg, beaten, to glaze

For the filling:
350 g/12 oz pork sausage meat
few drops Worcestershire
   sauce
salt and freshly ground
   black pepper

Preheat the oven to 220°C/425°F/Gas Mark 7. Lightly oil two baking sheets.

Sift the flour and salt into a bowl. Cut the fats into small pieces and add them to the bowl. Rub the fats into the flour using your fingertips, or place the flour and fats in a food processor and process, until the mixture resembles fine crumbs.

Mix together with 1–2 tablespoons cold water to make a soft but not sticky dough. Knead lightly until smooth, then wrap in clingfilm and chill for 30 minutes.

Season the sausage meat with the Worcestershire sauce, salt and pepper. Divide into four, then roll each piece into a 25 cm/10 inch length. Roll out the pastry on a floured surface to a rectangle 40 x 25 cm/16 x 10 inches and cut into four strips 10 cm/4 inches wide. Place one roll of sausage meat down the centre of each pastry strip. Brush the edge of the pastry with beaten egg, fold each one over the meat and seal.

Brush the top and sides with beaten egg, then cut each large roll into 3. Cut slashes through the tops and place the 12 sausage rolls on the prepared baking sheets. Bake for 10 minutes, then reduce the temperature to 190°C/375°F/Gas Mark 5 and bake for a further 15 minutes, or until light golden. Eat hot or cold. Will keep for 2 days in an airtight container in the fridge.

Bacon, Mushroom & Cheese Puffs

SERVES 4

1 tbsp olive oil
225 g/8 oz field mushrooms,
    wiped and roughly chopped
225 g/8 oz rindless streaky
    bacon, roughly chopped
2 tbsp freshly
    chopped parsley

salt and freshly ground
    black pepper
350 g/12 oz ready-rolled puff
    pastry sheets, thawed
    if frozen
25 g/1 oz Emmenthal
    cheese, grated

1 medium egg, beaten
salad leaves, such as rocket
    or watercress, to garnish
tomatoes, to serve

Preheat the oven to 200°C/400°F/Gas Mark 6. Heat the olive oil in a large frying pan. Add the mushrooms and bacon and fry for 6–8 minutes until golden in colour. Stir in the parsley, season to taste with salt and pepper and allow to cool.

Roll the sheet of pastry a little thinner on a lightly floured surface to a 30 cm/12 inch square. Cut the pastry into 4 equal squares.

Stir the grated Emmenthal cheese into the mushroom mixture. Spoon a quarter of the mixture onto one half of each square.

Brush the edges of the square with a little of the beaten egg. Fold over the pastry to form a triangular parcel. Seal the edges well and place on a lightly oiled baking sheet. Repeat until the squares are done.

Make shallow slashes in the top of the pastry with a knife. Brush the parcels with the remaining beaten egg and cook in the preheated oven for 20 minutes, or until puffy and golden brown.

Serve warm or cold, garnished with the salad leaves and served with tomatoes.

Classic Quiche Lorraine

SERVES 4–6

125 g/4 oz plain flour
pinch salt
25 g/1 oz white vegetable fat
25 g/1 oz butter

For the filling:
1 tsp vegetable oil

125 g/4 oz smoked streaky
    bacon, trimmed
    and chopped
75 g/3 oz Gruyère
    cheese, grated
2 medium eggs, beaten
150 ml/¼ pint single cream

1 tsp French mustard
tomatoes and green salad,
    to serve

Sift the flour and salt into a bowl. Cut the fats into small pieces and rub into the flour with your fingertips until the mixture resembles fine crumbs. If you have a food processor, process the fats and flour until the mixture forms fine crumbs.

Stir in enough cold water, about 1 tbsp, to form a soft dough. Wrap the dough in clingfilm and chill for 30 minutes. Preheat the oven to 180°C/350°F/Gas Mark 4, 10 minutes before baking and grease a 20.5 cm/8 inch flan tin.

Roll out the pastry to a circle large enough to line the tin. Press into the tin and up the sides. Prick the base lightly with a fork. Line the pastry with a large piece of nonstick baking parchment. Pour in some baking beans. Place in the oven and bake for 15 minutes. Remove the tin from the oven and carefully lift out the paper and beans.

Pour the oil into a nonstick pan over a medium heat. Add the bacon and fry for about 4 minutes until crisp and brown, then leave to cool. Scatter the bacon into the pastry case with the grated cheese. Whisk the eggs with the cream and mustard and pour carefully into the pastry case. Bake for 30–35 minutes until golden and firm in the centre. Serve hot or cold with tomatoes and a green salad. To serve cold, keeps 24 hours refrigerated.

Tomato & Courgette Herb Tart

SERVES 4

4 tbsp olive oil
1 onion, peeled and
    finely chopped
3 garlic cloves, peeled
    and crushed
400 g/14 oz prepared puff
    pastry, thawed if frozen

1 small egg, beaten
2 tbsp freshly
    chopped rosemary
2 tbsp freshly
    chopped parsley
175 g/6 oz rindless fresh soft
    goats' cheese

4 ripe plum tomatoes, sliced
1 medium courgette,
    trimmed and sliced
thyme sprigs, to garnish

Preheat the oven to 230°C/450°F/Gas Mark 8. Heat 2 tablespoons of the oil in a large frying pan. Fry the onion and garlic for about 4 minutes until softened and reserve.

Roll out the pastry on a lightly floured surface and cut out a 30 cm/12 inch circle. Brush the pastry with a little beaten egg, then prick all over with a fork. Transfer onto a dampened baking sheet and bake in the preheated oven for 10 minutes.

Turn the pastry over and brush with a little more egg. Bake for a further 5 minutes, then remove from the oven.

Mix together the onion, garlic and herbs with the goats' cheese and spread over the pastry.

Arrange the tomatoes and courgette over the goats' cheese and drizzle with the remaining oil.

Bake for 20–25 minutes until the pastry is golden brown and the topping is bubbling. Garnish with the thyme sprigs and serve immediately.

Potato & Goats' Cheese Tart

SERVES 6

275 g/10 oz prepared shortcrust pastry, thawed if frozen
550 g/1 lb 3 oz small waxy potatoes
beaten egg, for brushing

2 tbsp sun-dried tomato paste
¼ tsp chilli powder, or to taste
1 large egg
150 ml/¼ pint sour cream
150 ml/¼ pint milk
2 tbsp freshly snipped chives

salt and freshly ground black pepper
300 g/11 oz goats' cheese, sliced
salad and warm crusty bread, to serve

Preheat the oven to 190°C/375°F/Gas Mark 5, about 10 minutes before cooking. Roll the pastry out on a lightly floured surface and use to line a 23 cm/9 inch fluted flan tin. Chill in the refrigerator for 30 minutes.

Scrub the potatoes, place in a large saucepan of lightly salted water and bring to the boil. Simmer for 10–15 minutes until the potatoes are tender. Drain and reserve until cool enough to handle.

Line the pastry case with greaseproof paper and baking beans or crumpled foil and bake blind in the preheated oven for 15 minutes. Remove from the oven and discard the paper and beans or foil. Brush the base with a little beaten egg, then return to the oven and cook for a further 5 minutes. Remove from the oven.

Cut the potatoes into 1 cm/½ inch thick slices and reserve. Spread the sun-dried tomato paste over the base of the pastry case, sprinkle with the chilli powder, then arrange the potato slices on top in a decorative pattern.

Beat together the egg, sour cream, milk and chives, then season to taste with salt and pepper. Pour over the potatoes. Arrange the goats' cheese on top of the potatoes. Bake in the preheated oven for 30 minutes until golden brown and set. Serve immediately with salad and warm bread.

Garlic Wild Mushroom Galettes

SERVES 6

1 quantity quick flaky pastry
   (*see* page 28), chilled
1 onion, peeled
1 red chilli, deseeded
2 garlic cloves, peeled
275 g/10 oz mixed
   mushrooms, e.g. oyster,
   chestnut, morel, cep
   and chanterelle

25 g/1 oz butter
2 tbsp freshly chopped parsley
125 g/4 oz mozzarella
   cheese, sliced

To serve:
cherry tomatoes
mixed green salad leaves

Preheat the oven to 220°C/425°F/Gas Mark 7. On a lightly floured surface, roll out the chilled pastry very thinly. Cut out six 15 cm/6 inch circles and place on a lightly oiled baking sheet.

Thinly slice the onion, then divide into rings and reserve.

Thinly slice the chilli and slice the garlic into wafer-thin slivers. Add to the onions and reserve.

Wipe or lightly rinse the mushrooms. Halve or quarter any large mushrooms and keep the small ones whole.

Heat the butter in a frying pan and sauté the onion, chilli and garlic gently for about 3 minutes. Add the mushrooms and cook for about 5 minutes until beginning to soften. Stir the parsley into the mushroom mixture and drain off any excess liquid.

Pile the mushroom mixture onto the pastry circles within 5 mm/¼ inch of the edge. Arrange the sliced mozzarella cheese on top. Bake in the preheated oven for 12–15 minutes until golden brown and serve with the tomatoes and salad.

Mediterranean Tartlets

MAKES 12

175 g/6 oz plain flour
pinch salt
75 g/3 oz butter or
   block margarine

For the filling:
50 g/2 oz feta cheese,
   crumbled

50 g/2 oz mozzarella
   cheese, grated
2 spring onions, chopped
4 medium tomatoes,
   chopped, seeds removed
2 tbsp chopped fresh basil
3 medium eggs
2 tbsp milk

salt and freshly ground
   black pepper
green salad, to serve

Sift the flour and salt into a bowl. Cut the fat into small pieces and add to the bowl. Rub the fat into the flour using your fingertips, or place the flour and fat in a food processor and process, until the mixture resembles fine crumbs. Mix together with 1–2 tablespoons cold water to make a soft but not sticky dough. Knead lightly until smooth, then wrap in clingfilm and chill for 30 minutes.

Grease a 12-hole muffin tray. Roll out the pastry thinly on a floured surface and, using a 7.5 cm/3 inch round cutter, cut out 12 rounds. Use these to line the holes of the muffin tray, pressing the dough into the holes. Place the tray in the freezer for 5 minutes, or chill for 30 minutes.

Preheat the oven to 190°C/375°F/Gas Mark 5. Make the filling by mixing the cheeses, onions, tomatoes and basil in a bowl, then spoon the mixture into the pastry cases. In a jug, beat the eggs and milk together and season with salt and pepper.

Carefully spoon 2 tablespoons of the egg mixture into each pastry case on top of the cheese filling. Bake the tartlets for 20 minutes, or until the filling has set. Leave to cool in the tin for 5 minutes, then turn out to cool or serve warm with a fresh green salad.

Olive & Feta Parcels

MAKES 6

1 small red pepper
1 small yellow pepper
125 g/4 oz assorted marinated
    green and black olives

125 g/4 oz feta cheese
2 tbsp pine nuts,
    lightly toasted
6 sheets filo pastry

3 tbsp olive oil
sour cream and chive dip,
    to serve

Preheat the oven to 180°C/350°F/Gas Mark 4. Preheat the grill, then line the grill rack with foil.

Cut the peppers into quarters and remove the seeds. Place skin-side up on the foil-lined grill rack and cook under the preheated grill for 10 minutes, turning occasionally, until the skins begin to blacken. Place the peppers in a polythene bag and leave until cool enough to handle, then skin and thinly slice.

Chop the olives and cut the feta cheese into small cubes. Mix together the olives, feta, sliced peppers and pine nuts.

Cut 1 sheet of filo pastry in half, then brush with a little of the oil. Place a spoonful of the olive and feta mixture about one third of the way up the pastry. Fold over the pastry and wrap to form a square parcel, encasing the filling completely.

Place this parcel in the centre of the second half of the pastry sheet. Brush the edges lightly with a little oil, bring up the corners to meet in the centre and twist them loosely to form a purse Brush with a little more oil and repeat with the remaining filo pastry and filling.

Place the parcels on a lightly oiled baking sheet and bake in the preheated oven for 10–15 minutes until crisp and golden brown. Serve with the dip.

Three–Tomato Pizzas

SERVES 2-4

1 quantity pizza dough
   (*see* page 328)
3 plum tomatoes
8 cherry tomatoes
6 sun-dried tomatoes

pinch sea salt
1 tbsp freshly chopped basil
2 tbsp extra virgin olive oil
125 g/4 oz buffalo mozzarella
   cheese, sliced

freshly ground black pepper
fresh basil leaves, to garnish

Preheat the oven to 220°C/425°F/Gas Mark 7. Place a baking sheet into the oven to heat up.

Divide the prepared pizza dough into four equal pieces. Roll out one quarter of the pizza dough on a lightly floured board to form a 20.5 cm/8 inch round. Lightly cover the 3 remaining pieces of dough with clingfilm.

Roll out the other three pieces into rounds, one at a time. While rolling out any piece of dough, keep the others covered with the clingfilm.

Slice the plum tomatoes, halve the cherry tomatoes and chop the sun-dried tomatoes into small pieces. Place a few pieces of each type of tomato on each pizza base, then season to taste with the sea salt.

Sprinkle with the chopped basil and drizzle with the olive oil. Place a few slices of mozzarella on each pizza and season with black pepper.

Transfer the pizzas onto the heated baking sheet and cook for 15–20 minutes until the cheese is golden brown and bubbling. Garnish with the basil leaves and serve immediately.

Spinach, Pine Nut & Mascarpone Pizza

SERVES 2-4

For the basic pizza dough:
225 g/8 oz strong plain flour
½ tsp salt
¼ tsp quick-acting dried yeast
150 ml/¼ pint warm water
1 tbsp extra virgin olive oil

For the topping:
3 tbsp olive oil

1 large red onion, peeled
    and chopped
2 garlic cloves, peeled
    and finely sliced
450 g/1 lb frozen spinach,
    thawed and drained
salt and freshly ground
    black pepper
3 tbsp passata

125 g/4 oz mascarpone cheese
1 tbsp toasted pine nuts

Preheat the oven to 220°C/425°F/Gas Mark 7. Sift the flour and salt into a bowl and stir in the yeast. Make a well in the centre and gradually add the water and oil to form a soft dough. Knead the dough on a floured surface for about 5 minutes until smooth and elastic. Place in a lightly oiled bowl and cover with clingfilm. Leave to rise in a warm place for 1 hour.

Knock the pizza dough with your fist a few times, shape and roll out thinly on a lightly floured board. Place on a lightly floured baking sheet and lift the edge to make a little rim. Place another baking sheet into the preheated oven to heat up.

Heat half the oil in a frying pan and gently fry the onion and garlic until soft and starting to change colour.

Squeeze out any excess water from the spinach and chop finely. Add to the onion and garlic with the remaining olive oil. Season to taste with salt and pepper.

Spread the passata on the pizza dough and top with the spinach mixture. Mix the mascarpone with the pine nuts and dot over the pizza. Slide the pizza onto the hot baking sheet and bake for 15–20 minutes. Transfer to a large plate and serve immediately.

Roquefort, Parma & Rocket Pizza

SERVES 2-4

1 quantity pizza dough
(*see* page 328)

For the basic tomato sauce:
400 g can chopped tomatoes
2 garlic cloves, peeled
   and crushed
grated zest of ½ lime
2 tbsp extra virgin olive oil

2 tbsp freshly chopped basil
½ tsp sugar
salt and freshly ground
   black pepper

For the topping:
125 g/4 oz Roquefort cheese,
   cut into chunks
6 slices Parma ham

50 g/2 oz rocket
   leaves, rinsed
1 tbsp extra virgin olive oil
50 g/2 oz Parmesan cheese,
   freshly shaved

Preheat the oven to 220°C/425°F/Gas Mark 7. Roll the pizza dough out on a lightly floured board to form a 25.5 cm/10 inch round.

Lightly cover the dough and reserve while making the sauce. Place a baking sheet in the preheated oven to heat up.

Place all of the tomato sauce ingredients in a large heavy-based saucepan and slowly bring to the boil. Cover and simmer for 15 minutes, uncover and cook for a further 10 minutes until the sauce has thickened and reduced by half.

Spoon the tomato sauce over the shaped pizza dough. Place on the hot baking sheet and bake for 10 minutes.

Remove the pizza from the oven and top with the Roquefort and Parma ham, then bake for a further 10 minutes.

Toss the rocket in the olive oil and pile onto the pizza. Sprinkle with the Parmesan cheese and serve immediately.

Spicy Vegetable Slice

SERVES 4

50 g/2 oz butter, melted
6 large or 12 small sheets
    filo pastry

For the filling:
2 tbsp olive oil
1 garlic clove, crushed
1 red pepper, deseeded
    and sliced

1 onion, chopped
50 g/2 oz button mushrooms,
    wiped and quartered
1 tsp ground coriander
1 tsp paprika
175 g/6 oz cauliflower
    florets
75 g/3 oz French beans,
    trimmed and chopped

125 g/4 oz canned
    chickpeas, drained
125 g/4 oz feta
    cheese, crumbled
1 tbsp fresh coriander,
    chopped
50 g/2 oz flaked almonds
salt and freshly ground
    black pepper

First, make the filling by heating the oil in a large saucepan over a medium heat. Add the garlic, red pepper and onion and fry for 3 minutes to soften. Add the mushrooms, coriander and paprika and cook for 1 minute, stirring constantly, then turn the mixture into a bowl to cool. Place the cauliflower in a large pan of boiling salted water and cook for 5 minutes. Add the beans and cook for a further 2 minutes until the vegetables are just softened, then drain well and add to the bowl with the other vegetables and add the chickpeas. Cool completely, then add the cheese and half the almonds. Season to taste with salt and pepper.

Preheat the oven to 200°C/400°F/Gas Mark 6. Brush a large baking sheet with melted butter. Unfold the filo pastry. Lay out 1 large or 2 small sheets (keeping the remaining sheets covered with a damp tea towel until you need them), overlapping on the baking sheet with the sides extending onto the work surface. Brush the pastry with melted butter. Place another layer of filo on top and repeat buttering and layering with the remaining sheets. Spoon the filling down the centre of the pastry to 3 cm/1¼ inches of the short edge. Fold the short sides over the filling and then roll up the sides to enclose the filling and make a roll. Turn the roll over and place seam-side down on the baking sheet. Brush with melted butter and sprinkle over the remaining almonds. Decorate with scraps of buttered filo pastry. Bake for about 30 minutes until golden. Serve immediately, sliced, with a fresh green salad and tomatoes.

Smoked Haddock Tart

SERVES 6

For the shortcrust pastry:
150 g/5 oz plain flour
pinch salt
25 g/1 oz lard or white
    vegetable fat, cut into
    small cubes
40 g/1½ oz butter or hard
    margarine, cut into
    small cubes

For the filling:
225 g/8 oz smoked haddock,
    skinned and cubed
2 large eggs, beaten
300 ml/½ pint double cream
1 tsp Dijon mustard
freshly ground black pepper
125 g/4 oz Gruyère
    cheese, grated

1 tbsp freshly
    snipped chives

To serve:
lemon wedges
tomato wedges
fresh green salad leaves

Preheat the oven to 190°C/375°F/Gas Mark 5. Sift the flour and salt into a large bowl. Add the fats and mix lightly. Using the fingertips, rub into the flour until the mixture resembles breadcrumbs. Sprinkle 1 tablespoon of cold water into the mixture and, with a knife, start bringing the dough together. (It may be necessary to use the hands for the final stage.) If the dough does not form a ball instantly, add a little more water. Put the pastry in a polythene bag and chill for at least 30 minutes.

On a lightly floured surface, roll out the pastry and use to line an 18 cm/7 inch lightly oiled quiche or flan tin. Prick the base all over with a fork and bake blind in the preheated oven for 15 minutes.

Carefully remove the pastry from the oven and brush with a little of the beaten egg. Return to the oven for a further 5 minutes.

For the filling, place the fish in the pastry case, then beat together the eggs and cream. Add the mustard, black pepper and cheese and pour over the fish. Sprinkle with the chives and bake for 35–40 minutes until the filling is golden brown and set in the centre. Serve hot or cold with the lemon and tomato wedges and salad leaves.

Smoked Salmon Quiche

SERVES 6

225 g/8 oz plain flour
50 g/2 oz butter
50 g/2 oz white vegetable
   fat or lard
2 tsp sunflower oil
225 g/8 oz potato, peeled
   and diced
125 g/4 oz Gruyère
   cheese, grated

75 g/3 oz smoked
   salmon trimmings
5 medium eggs, beaten
300 ml/½ pint single cream
salt and freshly ground
   black pepper
1 tbsp freshly chopped
   flat-leaf parsley

To serve:
mixed salad
baby new potatoes

Preheat the oven to 200°C/400°F/Gas Mark 6. Blend the flour, butter and white vegetable fat or lard together until it resembles fine breadcrumbs. Blend again, adding sufficient water to make a firm but pliable dough. Use the dough to line a 23 cm/9 inch flan dish or tin, then chill the pastry case in the refrigerator for 30 minutes. Bake blind with baking beans for 10 minutes.

Heat the oil in a small frying pan, add the diced potato and cook for 3–4 minutes until lightly browned. Reduce the heat and cook for a further 2–3 minutes until tender. Leave to cool.

Scatter the grated cheese evenly over the base of the pastry case, then arrange the cooled potato on top. Add the smoked salmon in an even layer.

Beat the eggs with the cream and season to taste with salt and pepper. Whisk in the parsley and pour the mixture carefully into the dish.

Reduce the oven to 180°C/350°F/Gas Mark 4 and bake for about 30–40 minutes until the filling is set and golden. Serve hot or cold with a mixed salad and baby new potatoes.

Smoked Mackerel Vol–au–Vents

350 g/12 oz prepared
   puff pastry
1 small egg, beaten
2 tsp sesame seeds
225 g/8 oz peppered
   smoked mackerel,
   skinned and chopped

5 cm/2 inch piece cucumber
4 tbsp soft cream cheese
2 tbsp cranberry sauce
1 tbsp freshly
   chopped dill
1 tbsp finely grated
   lemon zest

dill sprigs, to garnish
mixed salad leaves, to serve

Preheat the oven to 230°C/450°F/Gas Mark 8. Roll the pastry out on a lightly floured surface and, using a 9 cm/3½ inch fluted cutter, cut out 12 rounds. Using a 1 cm/½ inch cutter, mark a lid in the centre of each round. Place on a damp baking sheet and brush the rounds with a little beaten egg.

Sprinkle the pastry with the sesame seeds and bake in the preheated oven for 10–12 minutes until golden brown and well risen.

Transfer the vol-au-vents to a chopping board and, when cool enough to touch, carefully remove the lids with a small sharp knife. Scoop out any uncooked pastry from the inside of each vol-au-vent, then return to the oven for 5–8 minutes to dry out. Remove and allow to cool.

Flake the mackerel into small pieces and reserve. Peel the cucumber if desired, cut into very small dice and add to the mackerel.

Beat the soft cream cheese with the cranberry sauce, dill and lemon zest. Stir in the mackerel and cucumber and use to fill the vol-au-vents. Place the lids on top and garnish with dill sprigs.

Sauvignon Chicken & Mushroom Filo Pie

SERVES 4

1 onion, peeled and chopped
1 leek, trimmed and chopped
225 ml/8 fl oz chicken stock
3 x 175 g/6 oz chicken breasts
150 ml/¼ pint dry white wine
1 bay leaf
175 g/6 oz baby
    button mushrooms

2 tbsp plain flour
1 tbsp freshly chopped
    tarragon
salt and freshly ground
    black pepper
fresh parsley sprig,
    to garnish
seasonal vegetables, to serve

For the topping:
75 g/3 oz (about 5 sheets)
    filo pastry
1 tbsp sunflower oil
1 tsp sesame seeds

Preheat the oven to 190°C/375°F/Gas Mark 5. Put the onion and leek in a heavy-based saucepan with 125 ml/4 fl oz of the stock. Bring to the boil, cover and simmer for 5 minutes, then uncover and cook until all the stock has evaporated and the vegetables are tender.

Cut the chicken into bite-size cubes. Add to the pan with the remaining stock, the wine and the bay leaf. Cover and gently simmer for 5 minutes. Add the mushrooms and simmer for a further 5 minutes.

Blend the flour with 3 tablespoons of cold water. Stir into the pan and cook, stirring all the time, until the sauce has thickened. Stir the tarragon into the sauce and season with salt and pepper. Spoon the mixture into a 1.2 litre/2 pint pie dish, discarding the bay leaf.

Lightly brush a sheet of filo pastry with a little of the oil. Crumple the pastry slightly. Arrange on top of the filling. Repeat with the remaining filo sheets and oil, then sprinkle the top of the pie with the sesame seeds. Bake the pie on the middle shelf of the preheated oven for 20 minutes until the filo pastry topping is golden and crisp. Garnish with a sprig of parsley. Serve the pie immediately with the seasonal vegetables.

Moroccan Lamb with Apricots

SERVES 6

5 cm/2 inch piece root ginger,
    peeled and grated
3 garlic cloves, peeled
    and crushed
1 tsp ground cardamom
1 tsp ground cumin
2 tbsp olive oil

450 g/1 lb lamb neck
    fillet, cubed
1 large red onion, peeled
    and chopped
400 g can chopped tomatoes
125 g/4 oz ready-to-eat
    dried apricots

400 g can chickpeas, drained
7 large filo pastry sheets
50 g/2 oz butter, melted
pinch nutmeg
dill sprigs, to garnish

Preheat the oven to 190°C/375°F/Gas Mark 5. Pound the ginger, garlic, cardamom and cumin to a paste with a pestle and mortar. Heat 1 tablespoon of the oil in a large frying pan and fry the spice paste for 3 minutes. Remove from the pan and reserve.

Add the remaining oil and fry the lamb in batches for about 5 minutes until golden brown. Return all the lamb to the pan and add the onion and the spice paste. Fry for 10 minutes, stirring occasionally. Add the chopped tomatoes, cover and simmer for 15 minutes. Add the apricots and chickpeas and simmer for a further 15 minutes.

Lightly oil a round 18 cm/7 inch springform cake tin. Lay 1 sheet of filo pastry in the base of the tin, allowing the excess to fall over the sides. Brush with melted butter, then layer 5 more sheets in the tin and brush each one with butter.

Spoon in the filling and level the surface. Layer half the remaining filo sheets on top, again brushing each with butter. Fold the overhanging pastry over the top of the filling. Brush the remaining sheet with butter, scrunch up and place on top of the pie so that the whole pie is completely covered. Brush with melted butter once more.

Bake in the preheated oven for 45 minutes, then reserve for 10 minutes. Unclip the tin and remove the pie. Sprinkle with the nutmeg, garnish with the dill sprigs and serve.

Cornish Pasties

MAKES 8

For the pastry:
350 g/12 oz self-raising flour
75 g/3 oz butter or margarine
75 g/3 oz lard or white
vegetable fat
salt and freshly ground
black pepper

For the filling:
550 g/1 lb 3 oz braising steak,
very finely chopped
1 large onion, peeled and
finely chopped
1 large potato, peeled
and diced

200 g/7 oz swede, peeled
and diced
3 tbsp Worcestershire sauce
1 small egg, beaten, to glaze

To garnish:
tomato slices or wedges
fresh parsley sprigs

Preheat the oven to 180°C/350°F/Gas Mark 4, about 15 minutes before required. To make the pastry, sift the flour into a large bowl and add the fats, chopped into small pieces. Rub the fats and flour together until the mixture resembles coarse breadcrumbs. Season to taste with salt and pepper and mix again. Add about 2 tablespoons of cold water, a little at a time, and mix until the mixture comes together to form a firm but pliable dough. Turn onto a lightly floured surface, knead until smooth, then wrap and chill in the refrigerator for 30 minutes.

To make the filling, put the braising steak in a large bowl with the onion. Add the potato and swede to the bowl, together with the Worcestershire sauce and salt and pepper. Mix well.

Divide the dough into 8 balls and roll each ball into a round about 25.5 cm/10 inches across. Divide the filling between the rounds of pastry. Wet the edges of the pastry, then fold over the filling. Pinch the edges to seal.

Transfer the pasties to a lightly oiled baking sheet. Make a couple of small holes in each pasty and brush with beaten egg. Cook in the preheated oven for 15 minutes, remove and brush again with the egg. Return to the oven for a further 15–20 minutes until golden. Cool slightly, garnish with tomato and parsley and serve.

Caribbean Empanadas

SERVES 4-6

175 g/6 oz lean fresh
   beef mince
175 g/6 oz lean fresh
   pork mince
1 onion, peeled and
   finely chopped
1 Scotch bonnet chilli,
   deseeded and
   finely chopped

1 small red pepper,
   deseeded and
   finely chopped
½ tsp ground cloves
1 tsp ground cinnamon
½ tsp ground allspice
1 tsp sugar
1 tbsp tomato purée
6 tbsp water

700 g/1½ lb prepared
   shortcrust pastry
   (*see* page 27)
melted butter, for brushing
lime wedges, to garnish
mango relish, to serve

Preheat the oven to 200°C/400°F/Gas Mark 6, 15 minutes before baking.

Place the mince in a nonstick frying pan and cook, stirring, for 5–8 minutes, or until sealed. Break up any lumps with a wooden spoon. Add the onion, chilli and red pepper together with the spices and cook, stirring, for 10 minutes, or until the onion has softened. Sprinkle in the sugar.

Blend the tomato purée with the water and stir into the meat. Bring to the boil, then reduce the heat and simmer for 10 minutes. Allow to cool.

Roll the pastry out on a lightly floured surface and cut into 10 cm/4 inch rounds. Place a spoonful of the meat mixture onto the centre of each pastry round and brush the edges with water. Fold over, encasing the filling to form small pasties.

Brush with melted butter and bake in the preheated oven for 20 minutes until golden. Garnish and serve with the mango relish.

Beef & Red Wine Pie

SERVES 4

700 g/1½ lb stewing
  beef, cubed
4 tbsp seasoned plain flour
2 tbsp sunflower oil
2 onions, peeled and chopped
2 garlic cloves, peeled
  and crushed

1 tbsp freshly
  chopped thyme
300 ml/½ pint red wine
150 ml/¼ pint beef stock
1–2 tsp Worcestershire sauce
2 tbsp tomato ketchup
2 bay leaves

knob butter
225 g/8 oz button
  mushrooms
1 quantity quick flaky pastry
  (*see* page 28), chilled
beaten egg or milk, to glaze
parsley sprig, to garnish

Preheat the oven to 200°C/400°F/Gas Mark 6. Toss the beef cubes in the seasoned flour.

Heat the oil in a large heavy-based frying pan. Fry the beef in batches for about 5 minutes until golden brown. Return all of the beef to the pan and add the onions, garlic and thyme. Fry for about 10 minutes, stirring occasionally. If the beef begins to stick, add a little water. Add the red wine and stock and bring to the boil. Stir in the Worcestershire sauce, tomato ketchup and bay leaves.

Cover and simmer on a very low heat for about 1 hour until the beef is tender. Heat the butter and gently sauté the mushrooms until golden brown. Add to the stew. Simmer uncovered for a further 15 minutes. Remove the bay leaves. Spoon the beef into a 1.1 litre/2 pint pie dish and reserve.

Roll out the pastry on a lightly floured surface. Cut out the lid to 5 mm/¼ inch wider than the dish. Brush the rim with the beaten egg and lay the pastry lid on top. Press to seal, then knock the edges with the back of a knife.

Cut a slit in the lid and brush with the beaten egg or milk to glaze. Bake in the preheated oven for 30 minutes, or until golden brown. Garnish with the sprig of parsley and serve immediately.

Index

A

All-in-one Chocolate Fudge Cakes 90
Almond & Cherry Cupcakes 112
Almond & Pine Nut Tart 236
Almond Cake 66
Almond Macaroons 176
apple
 Apple Pie 204
 Autumn Tart 234
 Baked Apple Dumplings 264
 Classic Apple Strudel 212
 Eve's Pudding 266
 Fruity Apple Tea Bread 306
 Toffee Apple Cake 62
Apple Pie 204
Autumn Tart 234

B

Bacon, Mushroom & Cheese Puffs 312
Baked Apple Dumplings 264
Baked Lemon & Sultana Cheesecake 224
Banana & Honey Tea Bread 304
Banana Cake 50
Banoffee Pie 220
beef
 Beef & Red Wine Pie 348
 Caribbean Empanadas 346
 Cornish Pasties 344
Beef & Red Wine Pie 348
Boys' & Girls' Names 134
Bread & Butter Pudding 254
Butterscotch Loaf 96

C

Cappuccino Muffins 126
Caramelised Chocolate Tartlets 246
Caribbean Empanadas 346
Carrot Cake 48
Chapattis 294
cheese
 Bacon, Mushroom & Cheese Puffs 312
 Cheese-crusted Potato Scones 302
 Goats' Cheese & Lemon Tart 232
 Olive & Feta Parcels 324
 Potato & Goats' Cheese Tart 318
 Roquefort, Parma & Rocket Pizza 330
 Spinach, Pine Nut & Mascarpone
  Pizza 328
Cheese-crusted Potato Scones 302
cherry
 Almond & Cherry Cupcakes 112
 Cherry Garlands 148
 Chocolate Chip Cherry Muffins 142
 Double Cherry Cupcakes 106
Cherry Garlands 148
Chestnut Cake 76
Chewy Choc & Nut Cookies 166
chocolate
 All-in-one Chocolate Fudge Cakes 90
 Caramelised Chocolate Tartlets 246
 Chewy Choc & Nut Cookies 166
 Chocolate & Cranberry Cupcakes 122
 Chocolate & Ginger Florentines 192
 Chocolate & Orange Rock Buns 94
 Chocolate & Toffee Cupcakes 124
 Chocolate & Vanilla Rings 162
 Chocolate Apricot Linzer Torte 244

Chocolate Brioche Bake 256
Chocolate Chip Cherry Muffins 142
Chocolate Chip Cookies 158
Chocolate Fruit Pizza 248
Chocolate Fudge Flake Cupcakes 120
Chocolate Lemon Tartlets 250
Chocolate Macaroons 200
Chocolate Mud Cupcakes 118
Chocolate Nut Brownies 92
Chocolate Orange Biscuits 198
Chocolate Pecan Angel Pie 252
Chocolate Pecan Pie 242
Easy Chocolate Cake 80
Fruit & Spice Chocolate Slice 100
Fudgy Chocolate Tiffin Bars 168
Honey & Chocolate Hearts 174
Mini Pistachio & Chocolate
 Strudels 214
Peach & Chocolate Bake 258
Shortbread Thumbs 184
Triple Chocolate Cheesecake 226
Triple Chocolate Muffins 128
White Chocolate Cookies 160
Chocolate & Cranberry Cupcakes 122
Chocolate & Ginger Florentines 192
Chocolate & Orange Rock Buns 94
Chocolate & Toffee Cupcakes 124
Chocolate & Vanilla Rings 162
Chocolate Apricot Linzer Torte 244
Chocolate Brioche Bake 256
Chocolate Chip Cherry Muffins 142
Chocolate Chip Cookies 158
Chocolate Fruit Pizza 248
Chocolate Fudge Flake Cupcakes 120

Chocolate Lemon Tartlets 250
Chocolate Macaroons 200
Chocolate Mud Cupcakes 118
Chocolate Nut Brownies 92
Chocolate Orange Biscuits 198
Chocolate Pecan Angel Pie 252
Chocolate Pecan Pie 242
Chocolate Pecan Traybake 86
Christmas Cake 56
Classic Apple Strudel 212
Classic Flapjacks 194
Classic Quiche Lorraine 314
Classic White Loaf 276
coconut
　Coconut Macaroons 178
　Moist Mocha & Coconut Cake 88
　Oatmeal Coconut Cookies 154
　Shaggy Coconut Cupcakes 114
Coconut Macaroons 178
coffee
　Cappuccino Muffins 126
　Coffee & Pecan Cake 84
　Coffee & Walnut Fudge Cupcakes 116
　Fudgy Mocha Pie with Espresso
　　Custard Sauce 228
　Moist Mocha & Coconut Cake 88
Coffee & Pecan Cake 84
Coffee & Walnut Fudge Cupcakes 116
College Pudding 270
Colourful Letters Cupcakes 132
Cornish Pasties 344
Crispy Rice Cakes 78
Crunchy Rhubarb Crumble 206
cupcakes
　Almond & Cherry Cupcakes 112
　Boys' & Girls' Names 134
　Chocolate & Cranberry Cupcakes 122
　Chocolate & Toffee Cupcakes 124
　Chocolate Fudge Flake Cupcakes 120
　Chocolate Mud Cupcakes 118
　Coffee & Walnut Fudge Cupcakes 116

　Colourful Letters Cupcakes 132
　Double Cherry Cupcakes 106
　Jellybean Cupcakes 136
　Madeleine Cupcakes 104
　Orange Drizzle Cupcakes 130
　Polka Dot Cupcakes 138
　Raspberry Butterfly Cupcakes 108
　Shaggy Coconut Cupcakes 114

D
Double Cherry Cupcakes 106
Drop Scones 70
Dundee Cake 54

E
Easy Chocolate Cake 80
Easy Danish Pastries 72
Easy Victoria Sponge 44
Eve's Pudding 266

F
Fat-free Sponge 46
fish
　Smoked Haddock Tart 334
　Smoked Mackerel Vol-au-Vents 338
　Smoked Salmon Quiche 336
Fondant Fancies 110
Freeform Fruit Pie 210
Fruit & Nut Flapjacks 196
Fruit & Spice Chocolate Slice 100
Fruit Cake 52
Fruity Apple Tea Bread 306
Fudgy Chocolate Tiffin Bars 168
Fudgy Mocha Pie with Espresso
　Custard Sauce 228

G
Garlic Wild Mushroom Galettes 320
ginger
　Chocolate & Ginger Florentines 192
　Ginger Snaps 190

　Gingerbread 68
　Gingerbread Biscuits 188
Ginger Snaps 190
Gingerbread 68
Gingerbread Biscuits 188
Goats' Cheese & Lemon Tart 232
Golden Castle Pudding 268
Golden Honey Fork Biscuits 172

H
honey
　Banana & Honey Tea Bread 304
　Golden Honey Fork Biscuits 172
　Honey & Chocolate Hearts 174
　Honey Cake 64
　Irish Soda Bread 282
　Spicy Filled Naan Bread 296
　Wholemeal Walnut Bread 280
Honey & Chocolate Hearts 174
Honey Cake 64
Hot Cross Buns 298

I
Iced Bakewell Tart 240
Irish Soda Bread 282

J
jam
　Almond & Pine Nut Tart 236
　Christmas Cake 56
　Chocolate Apricot Linzer Torte 244
　Easy Victoria Sponge 44
　Iced Bakewell Tart 240
　Jammy Buns 74
　Madeleine Cupcakes 104
　Mini Strawberry Tartlets 230
　Raspberry Butterfly Cupcakes 108
　Traffic Lights 146
　Viennese Fingers 182
Jammy Buns 74
Jellybean Cupcakes 136

L

Lattice Treacle Tart 238
lemon
  Baked Lemon & Sultana Cheesecake 224
  Chocolate Lemon Tartlets 250
  Goats' Cheese & Lemon Tart 232
  Lemon Butter Biscuits 150
  Lemon Drizzle Cake 58
  Lemon Meringue Pie 218
Lemon Butter Biscuits 150
Lemon Drizzle Cake 58
Lemon Meringue Pie 218
Luxury Mince Pies 260

M

Madeleine Cupcakes 104
Marble Cake 82
Marmalade Loaf Cake 98
'Mars' Bar Mousse in Filo Cups 216
Meditteranean Tartlets 322
Melting Moments 156
Mini Pistachio & Chocolate Strudels 214
Mini Strawberry Tartlets 230
Miracle Bars 170
Moist Mocha & Coconut Cake 88
Moroccan Lamb with Apricots 342
Multigrain Bread 278
mushroom
  Bacon, Mushroom & Cheese Puffs 312
  Garlic Wild Mushroom Galettes 320
  Sauvignon Chicken & Mushroom Filo Pie 340

N

nuts
  Almond & Cherry Cupcakes 112
  Almond & Pine Nut Tart 236
  Almond Cake 66
  Almond Macaroons 176
  Chestnut Cake 76
  Chewy Choc & Nut Cookies 166
  Chestnut Cake 76

Chocolate Nut Brownies 92
Chocolate Pecan Angel Pie 252
Chocolate Pecan Pie 242
Chocolate Pecan Traybake 86
Coffee & Pecan Cake 84
Coffee & Walnut Fudge Cupcakes 116
Dundee Cake 54
Fruit & Nut Flapjacks 196
Mini Pistachio & Chocolate Strudels 214
Miracle Bars 170
Peanut Butter Truffle Cookies 164
Pecan Caramel Millionaire's
  Shortbread 186
Pistachio Muffins 140
Spinach, Pine Nut & Mascarpone Pizza 328
Wholemeal Walnut Bread 280

O

Oatmeal Coconut Cookies 154
Oatmeal Raisin Cookies 152
Olive & Feta Parcels 324
orange
  Chocolate & Orange Rock Buns 94
  Chocolate Orange Biscuits 198
  Orange Drizzle Cupcakes 130
  Orange Fruit Cake 60
Orange Drizzle Cupcakes 130
Orange Fruit Cake 60

P

Peach & Chocolate Bake 258
Peanut Butter Truffle Cookies 164
Pecan Caramel Millionaire's Shortbread 186
Pistachio Muffins 140
Polka Dot Cupcakes 138
Poppy Seed Plait 290
Potato & Goats' Cheese Tart 318
Puff Pastry Jalousie 262

Q

Quick Brown Bread 274

R

Raspberry Butterfly Cupcakes 108
Rhubarb & Raspberry Cobbler 208
Ricotta Cheesecake with Strawberry
  Coulis 222
Roquefort, Parma & Rocket Pizza 330
Rosemary & Olive Focaccia 292

S

Sausage Rolls 310
Sauvignon Chicken & Mushroom Filo Pie 340
Shaggy Coconut Cupcakes 114
Shortbread Thumbs 184
Smoked Haddock Tart 334
Smoked Mackerel Vol-au-Vents 338
Smoked Salmon Quiche 336
Soft Dinner Rolls 284
Spicy Filled Naan Bread 296
Spicy Vegetable Slice 332
Spinach, Pine Nut & Mascarpone Pizza 328
Sweet Potato Baps 288

T

Three-Tomato Pizzas 326
Toffee Apple Cake 62
Tomato & Basil Rolls 286
Tomato & Courgette Herb Tart 316
Traditional Oven Scones 300
Traffic Lights 146
Triple Chocolate Cheesecake 226
Triple Chocolate Muffins 128

V

Viennese Fingers 182

W

Whipped Shortbread 180
White Chocolate Cookies 160
Wholemeal Walnut Bread 280